The
# Reference Shelf ®

# The American Dream

The Reference Shelf
Volume 90 • Number 5
H.W. Wilson
A Division of EBSCO Information Services, Inc.

Published by
**GREY HOUSE PUBLISHING**
Amenia, New York
2018

# The Reference Shelf

The books in this series contain reprints of articles, excerpts from books, addresses on current issues, and studies of social trends in the United States and other countries. There are six separately bound numbers in each volume, all of which are usually published in the same calendar year. Numbers one through five are each devoted to a single subject, providing background information and discussion from various points of view and concluding with an index and comprehensive bibliography that lists books, pamphlets, and articles on the subject. The final number of each volume is a collection of recent speeches. Books in the series may be purchased individually or on subscription.

Publisher's Cataloging-In-Publication Data
(Prepared by The Donohue Group, Inc.)

Names: Grey House Publishing, Inc., compiler.
Title: American Dream / [compiled by] Grey House Publishing.
Other Titles: Reference shelf ; v. 90, no. 5.
Description: Amenia, New York : Grey House Publishing, 2018. | Includes bibliographical references and index.
Identifiers: ISBN 9781682178683 (v. 90, no. 5) | ISBN 9781682177471 (volume set)
Subjects: LCSH: American Dream--Sources. | United States--Emigration and immigration--Sources. | Equality--United States--Sources. | Social mobility--United States--Sources. | Minorities--United States--Sources. | United States--Economic conditions--21st century--Sources. | National characteristics, American--Sources.
Classification: LCC E169.12 .A44 2018 | DDC 973--dc23

Printed in Canada

# Contents

# 3

## Race and the American Dream

# 4

## The American Dream Over Time

# 5

## Future of the Dream

# Preface

## What Is the American Dream?

The American dream is defined by *Merriam-Webster* as "a happy way of living that is thought of by many Americans as something that can be achieved by anyone in the U.S. especially by working hard and becoming successful."[1] This standard definition, however, doesn't fully encapsulate how the national credo of the American dream has captured the imagination of the American people and has become a source of pride for Americans living through the past century. Journalists and social analysts who examine the American dream in the twenty-first century, frequently look at how the concept changed over time, and explore how different groups of Americans have come to have different ideas about living the dream of being or becoming American.

The American dream says that hard work and talent are key. It says that any individual, no matter the circumstances of their birth, can advance to a better life in America. A 2012 *CNN Poll* found that about 42 percent of Americans believed that they would achieve the American dream, and a 2013 study from Gallup revealed that 43 percent of Americans believed that the average American doesn't have a chance of achieving the dream. When Gallup asked this question in 1952, only 8 percent of respondents felt that most Americans were unable to achieve the dream.[2] This increasing pessimism with regard to the promise and progress of American society dominates debates about American politics and the economy.

## Exploring the Dream

Given how deeply the concept of the American dream has become ingrained in the American mindset, it is not surprising that literacy scholars find symbolism and reflections of the American dream in many central works of American literature. One of the great American novels to reflect on the American dream is John Steinbeck's *Of Mice and Men*. Tracing the lives of two migrant workers living through the Great Depression, the novel illustrates perhaps the greatest single test of the American dream until the modern era. While other financial downturns impacted parts of America's upper classes, the stock market crash and the Depression that followed brought many Americans from the upper echelons to poverty. It was a frightening revelation that forced the American people and government to recognize that America's free market was not as infallible as many had long believed.

One of the factors that contributed to the Depression was a drought that hit the Great Plains region of the United States between 1930 and 1940. The drought was, in part, the result of human factors, namely the great farming boom in the central plains, not unlike to how the burning of fossil fuels is today causing droughts and natural disasters as the planet warms. In 1930, when the natural drought cycle hit the plains, nineteen states in the interior United States became so parched that they were colloquially called the "Dust Bowl." Tens of thousands of farmers and laborers were out of work and, in desperation, migrated across the country searching for any chance at employment.[3] John Steinbeck became America's great literary chronicler of the Dust Bowl, primarily through his novel *The Grapes of Wrath*, which documented the plight of migrant families during the Depression.

Both *Of Mice and Men* and *The Grapes of Wrath* explore the themes of migrant labor, and how the dream of a better life carries the characters through the ruined landscape created by the Great Depression. Though a relatively humble version of the American dream, the characters' desire to escape the financial struggle of the lower class reflects the essence of the dream in its myriad forms.

Ultimately, as the characters are unable to realize their dream, Steinbeck thus portrays the American dream as a forever elusive goal for those starting at the bottom level.

## Class and the American Dream

It is no secret that Americans are increasingly skeptical about the American dream. With rising income inequality and problems relating to wage stagnation and economic mobility, fewer Americans are managing to ascend the economic ladder, and fewer are earning more or advancing to higher levels of prosperity than their parents. Partly due to increasing government distrust, as well as the perception of inequality in America, there is an increasing perception that the American dream is off track, or even dead.

Another American literature classic, F. Scott Fitzgerald's *The Great Gatsby*, is set during the 1920s, before the phrase "American dream" came into widespread usage. Writing in the *Guardian* in 2013, journalist Nikki Lusk writes that the 1925 novel "lays bare the moral vacuity at the heart of the American Dream," which draws attention to a "glittering façade" that crumbles before one's eyes. The novel follows Nick Carraway, a young Ivy League graduate who becomes embroiled in the playboy lifestyle of self-made Midwestern millionaire Jay Gatsby, a symbol of how the race for wealth and status is meretricious, encouraging Americans to seek hollow goals and, further, to leave behind more fulfilling aspects of their lives in pursuit of wealth as an end.

In 2012, economist Alan Krueger, chairman of the president's Council of Economic Advisers, identified the "Great Gatsby Curve." He pointed out a causal correlation between economic mobility and equality. What this means is that countries in which parental income is a major factor in the success of children are less equal societies. According to Krueger, the United States is becoming one of the poorest countries based on economic mobility, reflected America's economic inequality. He warned that, given current economic trends, income inequality is growing, with more of the nation's wealth concentrated at the top of the income spectrum, out of reach for the majority of Americans[4] and labeled his economic theory after *The*

*Great Gatsby* because he believed that income inequality in America had risen to the highest level since the 1920s (the setting for the novel). The "roaring" 20s were a time of liberalism, with Americans celebrating the end of the Great War with a renewed focus on getting their share of the American dream. The decade saw an unprecedented number of "get-rich-quick" schemes, which either amounted to little, or were swindles like the now-famous scheme by Boston's Charles Ponzi, named in his honor, as well as an unprecedented explosion of high-stakes gambling. This reflected a new ethos in America -- a singular focus on accumulating wealth and materialism, the likes of which had not been seen before. There were few protections preventing companies from creating monopolies or exploiting the public for profit, and few safety nets in place to help those whose gambles didn't pay off.

The growing obsession with wealth that characterized the 1920s, coupled with unrestrained and largely unregulated growth of business and the competitive hunger for profit were, to the nation's economy and the populations of America's cities, what the unsustainable farming and ranching practices were to America's Great Plains. Just as the Great Plains, stripped of the grasses, wildflowers, and shrubs that held the soil in place, became a dust-filled wasteland when the great drought arrived, the American economy suffered the same in the stock market crash of 1929 that led into the Great Depression.

James Truslow Adams, the man who popularized the phrase "American dream" in his 1931 book *The American Epic*, was a champion of the idea that America provided a unique "social order" that promoted success. While Adams believed in America, he also felt that Americans had betrayed this hope. Writing in the *New York Times* in 1933, responding in part to the debate his book had inspired among economists and the public, Adams argued:

> Throughout our history, the pure gold of this vision has been heavily alloyed with the dross of materialistic aims. Not only did the wage scales and our standard of living seem to promise riches to the poor immigrant, but the extent and natural wealth of the continent awaiting exploitation offered to Americans of the older stocks such opportunities for rapid fortunes that the making of money and the enjoying of what money could buy too often became our ideal of a full and satisfying life. The struggle of each against all for the dazzling prizes destroyed in some measure both our private ideals and our sense of social obligation.[5]

## A Nonexistent Dream?

Critics of the American dream, like Steinbeck, Fitzgerald, and even Adams, saw a dream that had been misinterpreted and degraded into little more than a contest for wealth. Within those criticisms, however, it is implied that America, because of its diversity and other unique qualities, has the potential to become a more egalitarian society.

And, of course, the dream is not the same for everyone. One's relationship with the dream depends on where one sits in the income spectrum, whether by birth or hard work. Access to the dream is also tied into race, with America's minorities often facing a different reality when climbing economic and social ladders. The American dream is changing, and each generation of Americans faces a different set of challenges in realizing their own version of success. In the twenty-first century, the rise of digital technology and the increasingly global market present their own economic challenges.

In many ways, too, the American dream is illusory. In most societies around the world, people struggle to realize their own sense of fulfillment, which are often not terribly different from the struggles that Americans face, although our nation's material wealth provides the possibility of advancement to levels that might be impossible in some other societies. The dream is not, therefore, a feature of American society as much as of the American mind. For some, the dream is a source of pride or a manifestation of patriotic impulses. For others, the dream is a motivator or a muse driving their efforts toward personal fulfillment. For still others, the dream is a dispiriting myth or a failed promise of a perennially elusive goal.

Micah L. Issitt

## Works Used

"The American Dream." *Merriam-Webster*. Merriam-Webster, Inc. 2018. Retrieved from https://www.merriam-webster.com/dictionary/the%20American%20dream.

Bowman, Karlyn, Marsico, Jennifer K., and Heather Sims. "Public Opinion and the American Dream." *AEI*. American Enterprise Institute. Dec 15, 2014. Retrieved from http://www.aei.org/publication/public-opinion-american-dream/.

Churchwell, Sarah. "The Great Gatsby and the American Dream." *The Guardian*. The Guardian News and Media. May 25, 2012. Retrieved from https://www.theguardian.com/books/2012/may/25/american-dream-great-gatsby.

"The Dust Bowl." Great Depression and World War I. *LOC*. Library of Congress. 2016. Retrieved from https://www.loc.gov/teachers/classroommaterials/presentationsandactivities/presentations/timeline/depwwii/dustbowl/.

Lisca, Peter. "Of Mice and Men." In Hobby, Blake, ed. *The American Dream*. New York: Bloom's Literary Criticism, 2009.

"Public Trust in Government: 1958-2017." *Pew Research*. Pew Research Center. Dec 14, 2017. Retrieved from http://www.people-press.org/2017/12/14/public-trust-in-government-1958-2017/.

Vandiver, David. "What Is the Great Gatsby Curve?" *Obamawhitehouse*. The White House. Jun 11, 2013. Retrieved from https://obamawhitehouse.archives.gov/blog/2013/06/11/what-great-gatsby-curve.

## Notes

1. "The American Dream," *Merriam-Webster*.
2. Bowman, Marsico, and Sims, "Public Opinion and the American Dream."
3. "The Dust Bowl," *LOC*.
4. Vandiver, "What Is the Great Gatsby Curve?"
5. Churchwell, "The Great Gatsby and the American Dream."

# 1
# Immigration

Anti-immigration activists assert that immigrants threaten the achievement of the American Dream for those who already live in the United States. Latin Americans and Muslims are the current targets of such campaigns, as were Catholics, the Irish, and Chinese laborers in previous eras. Here, future citizens take part in a naturalization ceremony at Oakton High School in Fairfax County, Virginia, December 2015.

# The Dream of Becoming American

Immigration created the American dream. It was the dream of wealth, prosperity, and freedom that drew the first colonists to the United States and the dream of a better life is what continues to draw millions of migrants to America each year. A popular saying among immigrants in the 1800s was "America beckons, but Americans repel," and this idiom captures the conflicting nature of immigration in the United States. From the beginning, immigrants were blamed for social and cultural problems, and used as a scapegoat by politicians. For immigrants and the native-born, the American dream therefore takes on multiple meanings; the dream that brings immigrants to the United States, and the dream of America as a nation of immigrants.

## Land of Opportunity

Over the centuries, immigrants have come to the United States for many different reasons. Some came to avoid war, crime, or persecution, others to escape governmental or military oppression, and still others came seeking freedom of religion. A main reason, however, is the opportunity to create personal wealth.

The United States is unique in that the massive, resource-rich nation was founded comparatively recently to the great societies of Europe, Asia, or the Middle East. By the time the first European colonists set foot on American soil, thousands of years of growth had left Europe's natural resources under the control of powerful elites and monarchic governments. In the United States, the wealth of natural resources, coupled with a technologically underdeveloped native population, created an open field for enterprising Europeans to exploit the environment for profit. The almost frenetic growth of the American colonies created a dire need for skilled services of many kinds and millions of immigrants came to take advantage of the expanding market. Fueled by word of mouth and writings spread over the seas, the American experiment captivated Europeans looking for change, new opportunities, and economic adventure, but, more than anything else, the nation became a beacon for those languishing in economic stagnation.

The mythological history of U.S. immigration depicts immigrants as representing the poor and downtrodden of the world's population and portrays the Golden Age of Migration (from about 1830-1920) as a flood of immigrants fleeing European tyranny and lured to the United States by the promise of freedom. In general, this was not the case. In fact, the nation's first immigration controversy came in the 1790s, when Alexander Hamilton and his fellow Federalists crafted new restrictive immigration policies intended to, among other things, discourage the immigration of the poor.[1]

3

Despite being lauded as the downtrodden immigrant's hero in the popular musical *Hamilton*, the real Alexander Hamilton was both anti-immigrant and pro-immigrant, depending on who the immigrant was. What Hamilton wanted was to allow the immigration of the wealthy, individuals he saw as having the appropriate skills and intelligence to contribute to the nation. This basic premise remains popular, such as in the 2017-2018 debate over "merit based" immigration. In his day, Hamilton very much saw America as the bastion of the "self-made" entrepreneur, but knew that the transition from pauper to millionaire was unrealistic. Instead, he wished to welcome those who already had a leg up, and so could more easily contribute to the prosperity of the growing nation.

Thus, rather than the poor, desperate, huddled masses of the world, it was more typically semiskilled laborers or artisans who came to the United States, as individuals in this demographic could better afford to make the journey. A study of Italian immigration, for instance, revealed that most of the Italian migrants who came to operate homesteads in the American west owned homesteads in Italy before making the migration and were thus already among the land-owning class before their arrival.

Because the allure of America was primarily financial, rather than cultural, many of the immigrants who came to the United States during the Golden Age of Migration were actually temporary migrants who hoped to come, earn their fortunes, and return home to their native countries and families. More than half of Italian immigrants, for instance, returned to Italy after living and working in the United States, as did 64 percent of Hungarians, 40 percent of Germans, and more than half of all Scandinavians. In fact, a full 30 percent of all immigrants arriving in the country during the golden age of migration were "birds of flight," who came to exploit America's riches, but did not make America their home.[2]

In the twenty-first century, the forces driving immigration are much the same. Of the millions of Latin American migrants who come to the United States, most come seeking to profit from the nation's comparatively robust economy. Many Latin American migrants come alone, leaving their children and families behind, and send money and other valuables, called "remittances," to their families back home. Not only does this provide a way for a worker to earn more than he or she might earn in a developing economy, but the resources sent back to those still living outside the nation can be incredibly impactful. Studies have shown that the money sent by Mexican migrants to poor communities in Mexico helps to reduce crime and alleviate poverty, and that families receiving remittances are more likely to afford essential services, like medical care and home improvement, than those subsisting on local wages. Through remittances, the wealth of the United States becomes a transformative force that can improve the lives of people living in poverty in developing communities. In 2016 alone, Latin American migrants in the United States sent more than $69 billion in remittances to family and friends in their native nations.[3]

For immigrants, the American dream has always been about a "better life," and not necessarily about becoming or being American.

However, even as opportunism fueled American growth, millions of migrants who came to the United States remained, setting up communities and integrating into American culture. While most immigrants do not climb the economic ladder from the working class to the middle class or from the middle to the upper, second-generation immigrants frequently move past their immigrant parents in terms of earnings and wealth. A person who spends their formative years in America is, in a very real sense, American. Over time, immigrants became American and the nation truly became a combination of cultures. This unique cultural mélange also became a cherished characteristic of American culture for many Americans as well and transformed the American dream from one in which the nation was a land of economic opportunity to a more philosophical view of America as a nation where cultures combine to create a new, emergent identity.

## The Anti-Immigrant Tradition

It is no exaggeration to say that America's status as a nation, its wealth, and its identity was created by immigration. Consider, for instance, that more than 25 percent of the soldiers who fought in the Union Army during the Civil War were foreign-born, despite the fact that the foreign-born constituted only 13 percent of the nation at that point. Together with native-born soldiers whose parents were foreign-born, immigrants (first or second generation) made up nearly half (43 percent) of the U.S. armed forces in the struggle that established the nation as *united* states.[4] There is no doubt that the nation would have had a much more difficult time becoming a leading world economy if the nation's population growth was based on reproduction alone, or if America's growth was based on native *innovation* alone. Over 40 percent of America's Fortune 500 firms were founded by immigrants or the children of immigrants and, per capita, America's resident immigrants found more new businesses than the native-born by a wide margin. Immigrant-owned businesses employ 5.9 million workers and contribute well over $65 billion in annual business income.[5] In short, immigrants continue to generate massive revenues that spread through society and continue to add cultural and social innovation to U.S. culture.

However, even as "America beckoned," there have always been some Americans that repelled.

Typically, in each generation, there is a target immigrant group that is singled out and designated as dangerous to America's economy or culture, from anti-Catholic sentiment in the early 1800s, to the "green menace" of Irish immigrants in the 1830s and 40s, then Chinese laborers in the 1850s, and in the 1920s a policy that essentially banned all nonwhite immigration, which did not end until the mid 1960s.

In the 2010s, anti-immigrant activists target Latin Americans and Muslims claiming that Latin American migrants are a drain on the economy and increase crime rates and that Muslim immigrants might conduct terrorist attacks in the United States, or/and that the Muslim religion and philosophy is incompatible with American culture. These same arguments were made about Catholic immigrants in the 1810s, Irish immigrants in the 1830s, and Chinese immigrants in the 1880s.

The American dream for immigrants has always been complicated by America's love/hate relationship with immigration. In general, anti-immigration sentiment is fueled primarily by racial prejudice and xenophobia, exacerbated by the fact that "issue entrepreneurs," individuals who capitalize on emerging issues for personal gain, fuel anti-immigrant anger as a way to obtain political or social power.

## A Nation of Immigrants

It wasn't until the 1960s that people started calling America a "nation of immigrants," which was a phrase derived from John F. Kennedy's 1960s book of the same name in which Kennedy argued that America's greatness was because of the nation's cultural diversity. Whether speaking philosophically or more pragmatically, America is and has always been a nation of immigrants, but the experience that immigrants face, and so the nature of the American dream for the nation's immigrant arrivals, changes from generation to generation, and depending on where and towards whom the nation's anti-immigration activists are focused.

## Works Used

Aizenman, Nurith. "Mexicans in the U.S. Are Sending Home More Money Than Ever." *NPR*. National Public Radio. Feb 10, 2017. Retrieved from https://www.npr.org/sections/goatsandsoda/2017/02/10/514172676/mexicans-in-the-u-s-are-sending-home-more-money-than-ever.

Chang, Gordon H., and Shelley Fisher Fishkin. "'The Chinese Helped Build America'." *Forbes*. Forbes Inc. May 12, 2014. Retrieved from https://www.forbes.com/sites/forbesasia/2014/05/12/the-chinese-helped-build-america/#77ab0f7339bc.

"The Chinaman as a Railroad Builder." *Scientific American*. Munn & Company. July 31, 1869, 75.

"Chinese Railroad Workers." *Stanford University*. FAQs. Retrieved from http://web.stanford.edu/group/chineserailroad/cgi-bin/wordpress/faqs/.

Coleman, Arica L. "The Problem with Calling the U.S. a 'Nation of Immigrants'." *Time*. Time Inc. Mar 17, 2017. Retrieved from http://time.com/4705179/nation-of-immigrants-problem/.

Connor, Phillip. "Most Displaced Syrians Are in the Middle East, and about a Million Are in Europe." *Pew Research*. Facttank. Jan 29, 2018. Retrieved from http://www.pewresearch.org/fact-tank/2018/01/29/where-displaced-syrians-have-re-settled/.

Diaz, Thatiana. "U.S. Citizenship Director Who Removed Phrase 'Nation of Immigrants' Is *Actually* Son of Immigrant." *People*. People Inc. Feb 27, 2018. Retrieved from https://people.com/chica/uscis-director-who-changed-mission-statement-is-son-of-peruvian-immigrant/.

Doyle, Don H. "The Civil War Was Won by Immigrant Soldiers." *Time*. Time Inc. Jun 29, 2015. Retrieved from http://time.com/3940428/civil-war-immigrant-soldiers/.

Frank, Jason, and Isaac Kramnick. "What 'Hamilton' Forgets About Hamilton." *The New York Times*. The New York Times Co. Jun 10, 2016. Retrieved from https://www.nytimes.com/2016/06/11/opinion/what-hamilton-forgets-about-alexander-hamilton.html.

"Nearly 6 Million Workers Employed at Immigrant-Owned Businesses, New Report Finds." *New American Economy*. Research Fund. Oct 11, 2016. Retrieved from https://research.newamericaneconomy.org/report/nearly-6-million-workers-employed-at-immigrant-owned-businesses-new-report-finds/.

Nowrasteh, Alex. "The 14 Most Common Arguments against Immigration and Why They're Wrong." *Cato Institute*. Cato at Liberty. May 2, 2018. Retrieved from https://www.cato.org/blog/14-most-common-arguments-against-immigration-why-theyre-wrong.

"Transcript of Alien and Sedition Acts (1798)." *Our Documents*. Yale University Library. Retrieved from https://www.ourdocuments.gov/doc.php?flash=false&doc=16&page=transcript.

Zeitz, Joshua. "The Real History of American Immigration." *Politico Magazine*. Politico. Aug 6, 2017. Retrieved from https://www.politico.com/magazine/story/2017/08/06/trump-history-of-american-immigration-215464.

## Notes

1. Frank and Kramnick, "What 'Hamilton' Forgets about Hamilton."
2. Zeitz, "The Real History of American Immigration."
3. Aizenman, "Mexicans in the U.S. Are Sending Home More Money Than Ever."
4. Doyle, The Civil War Was Won by Immigrant Soldiers."
5. "Nearly 6 Million Workers Employed at Immigrant-Owned Businesses, New Report Finds," *New American Economy*.

# For the Child of Immigrants, the American Dream Can Be a Nightmare

By Karla Cornejo Villavicencio
*Vogue*, April 17, 2018

This is a story about love and sacrifice in the shining city on a hill. It is about the wildest, blindest love story in America, the story of the devotion immigrants have for a country that wants to expel them. This love perseveres past heartbreak; past giving your body, mind, and youth to a country you risked your life to get to, then seeing your own tax money pay for immigration officials to pursue an ambulance carrying a 10-year-old girl with cerebral palsy on the way to emergency surgery just to detain her and send her to a detention shelter without her caretakers. The curly-haired father who faces violent gangs in his home country: gone. The 5-year-old American citizen who believed his father (who is hiding in a church to give his lawyers more time to fight a deportation order) is just at work and he'll come home soon: ICE makes no exception for them either. They used to have the decency of knocking down our doors in the middle of the night. It was scary and humiliating, but it was tonally appropriate—it was violence that felt violent. There was the illusion that the reason they were getting away with it was because it was dark; polite society was asleep. Now they are disappearing us in the middle of the day, in front of schools and hospitals and courthouses. Many of the children of these targeted migrants are American citizens. Do you believe, under the circumstances, that this love story could be true?

For the past year, I've been researching my forthcoming book, *Undocumented America*, in which I recount the intimate stories of undocumented immigrants throughout the United States. Regardless of their circumstances, they all have one thing in common—the looming threat of deportation. In early 2017, John Kelly (now President Trump's chief of staff, but then head of the Department of Homeland Security) issued memos doing away with many Obama-era enforcement priorities, meaning targets for deportation not only included criminals and security risks but overnight became anyone and everyone. Minors and the parents and spouses of American citizens were suddenly in the crosshairs—and it is no exaggeration to say that in this current moment, immigrants are being hunted like animals. Yet when we talk about who deserves protection from this policy, we only talk about Dreamers— undocumented immigrants who arrived in the States as children and who had been given safe harbor here under DACA (Deferred Action for Childhood Arrivals). What about those children's parents, the protagonists of that original love story?

I am one of those children. And I know that love story like the back of my hand.

I was 5 years old when I arrived in New York City from Ecuador. During that first summer in America, my undocumented parents took me to Times Square, the Empire State Building, the Twin Towers, Central Park, Bloomingdale's window displays, the Bronx Zoo, Coney Island. "This is America," they said, spreading their arms wide. I learned about America at home, too. Although my family was poor when I was a kid, my mother's closet has always been filled with vintage dresses from secondhand stores. She loves dresses that cinch at the waist and flare out extravagantly, and she collects pillbox hats, mink shawls, white dinner gloves, tiny clutches, and gilded brooches. Before she learned the word *vintage*, she called these dresses "from a time before." In context: "Daughter, I need a floral dress from a time before to wear to church." The vagueness annoyed me. I told her that could mean anything from the early Neanderthal period to the Middle Ages. But she would just hum Frank Sinatra as she twirled in her dresses, because we both knew what she meant. She meant the same thing old white racists who want America to "return" to greatness now mean—an imagined snapshot of an anonymous suburb in the 1950s. A Norman Rockwell painting where a girl in a poodle skirt shares a milkshake with a blond boy with a cowlick. *A time before.*

Once, for a wedding, my mother sewed me into a baby blue chiffon prom dress from the 1960s, hemmed to conceal a stain. I couldn't breathe in the dress, but I looked like a vision of who she wanted me to be. *White.* My mother may not have wanted me to *be* white, but she feared what would happen to me when the world realized I wasn't. She had big dreams for me. A stay-at-home mom until recently, she told me, when I was little, that I needed to be a career woman; that way, I'd never have to extend my hand to a man to ask for money. America for her means fully empowered womanhood. When she sees glamorous, successful women on TV, women like Hillary Clinton or Condoleezza Rice, she whispers, "I wonder what it feels like to be a successful woman." Then she pauses for a moment before she turns to me, her voice turning sharp, as she says: "That's why we stayed, you know. So you could be a successful woman. I live through you."

While my mom stayed at home, my dad was on the front lines of America as an immigrant, working in the restaurant industry. He faced racist abuse, wage theft, devastating humiliation, xenophobia, grueling manual labor, poor pay. My father has always had the rhetorical style of a Latin American dictator, which is to say wordy, and has also been excessively prone to metaphor. America to him has always meant two different sports—baseball, and soccer. He watched Babe Ruth documentaries all the time and sought out biographies about the baseball star from the library. He

> **I have excelled in this country; I am so very much the American Dream that I should be bottled and sold.**

admired Ruth for his bootstrap story. Over time, he became obsessed with the New York Yankees and taught himself to understand the rules of baseball. He started taking me to games, buying tickets for seats in the nosebleed section, and once he brought me home a laminated photo of the captain at the time, the legendary No. 2, Derek Jeter, that he purchased from a man on the street. When my little brother was born in November 1998, the Yankees were playing in the World Series. My brother is named Derek.

For my father, baseball seemed like the purest form of assimilation. But he was obsessive about teaching me about another sport, too. He told me that, in America, our family was a soccer team. We all had roles. His position was defense. I was the star kicker. He would protect me and, in turn, I would be my family's face in the world, bearing both of my parents' last names. Cornejo, his. Villavicencio, hers. My mother and father worked hard behind the scenes so I could shine on the field, so I could be a Latin American team making goal after goal against their colonial rulers—Portugal, Spain, or England. In Ecuador, my father had been such a talented soccer player that his nickname was Ronaldinho, after the Brazilian soccer star. In America, he passed on the crown to me. Whenever I had a standardized exam or a job interview or was working on an album review for the local jazz newspaper, he would say, "Your team is behind you. Make the goal." I've made goal after goal for 25 years and it's made my parents proud. But do you want to know something? Pride don't mean shit.

I never identified as a Dreamer. First, I thought the acronym was cheesy. Second, I feel sick at the thought of the American public pitying me for my innocence, my hands clean from my parents' purported sin in bringing me here. It's a self-righteous position I want to kick in the balls—pitying the child while accusing the parents of doing something that any other good parent would have done under the same circumstances. And if American citizens' love of law and order is so pure that they would have let their children rot or starve or be shot or be condemned to a future of no future instead of coming here, then they're not fit to shine my parents' shoes.

My parents are quick to identify as American. They go to the Fourth of July fireworks by the Brooklyn Bridge every year and root for the U.S. in the Olympics. In public, my mother says her favorite book is the Bible, but it is actually Hillary Clinton's *Living History*. She has entire passages memorized. (My mother idolized Hillary from the moment she laid eyes on her, which was shortly after a young Bill Clinton shook hands with my mother at a campaign stop in Brooklyn. When Hillary wore headbands, my mother wore headbands. When she forgave Bill, my mother did, too.) My parents train for 5Ks together. On weekends, they go to the Union Square farmers' market or to Chinatown for dumplings, like any other New Yorkers. My relationship with America is a little more complicated than theirs. I have not inherited the cognitive dissonance necessary to unconditionally love something that hates you, and I am childless—I have dogs, not kids—so I don't take consolation in the hope that my children will reap what I sow, that I will plant seeds that will bear fruit my children will eat. This all ends with me.

The twisted inversion that many children of immigrants know is that, at some point, your parents become your children, and your own personal American dream is making sure they age and die with dignity in a country that has never wanted them. I have excelled in this country; I am so very much the American Dream that I should be bottled and sold—but the parents who brought me forth, who are responsible for everything from my lovely Catholic school cursive to my commitment to philanthropy, are being persecuted like the rest of the 11 million undocumented immigrants who have laid down roots in the country they love and who now face a painful expulsion. When I watched my parents watching the Winter Olympics this year, the pair of them in front of the television, their hands over their hearts and their eyes sparkling with pride for the athletes on-screen, my eyes were only on them and my heart was in my throat. My allegiance, as ever, is to them; they are the country that I love. What makes me American—what makes the children of immigrants American in the most fundamental of ways—is something we learned from watching how unkindly America has treated our mothers and fathers. Our entire lives have been spent trying to deserve America. America needs to earn us, too.

## Print Citations

**CMS:** Cornejo Villavicencio, Karla. "For the Child of Immigrants, the American Dream Can Be a Nightmare." In *The Reference Shelf: The American Dream,* edited by Annette Calzone, 9-12. Ipswich, MA: H.W. Wilson, 2018.

**MLA:** Cornejo Villavicencio, Karla. "For the Child of Immigrants, the American Dream Can Be a Nightmare." In *The Reference Shelf: The American Dream.* Ed. Annette Calzone. Ipswich: H.W. Wilson, 2018. 9-12. Print.

**APA:** Cornejo Villavicencio, K. (2018). For the child of immigrants, the American dream can be a nightmare. In Annette Calzone (Ed.), *The reference shelf: The American Dream* (pp. 9-12). Ipswich, MA: H.W. Wilson. (Original work published 2018)

# Reunited, an Immigrant Family Tries to Put Their Life Back Together

By Jonathan Blitzer
*The New Yorker*, August 1, 2018

Last Friday morning, I had breakfast with a Honduran woman named Wendy Santos and her two daughters, Valeria and Aleisha, in the kitchen of their new home in suburban Maryland. Aleisha, who is three, was playing a game she recently invented for herself. "Copy, copy," she said, looking at us, expectantly. She slid off her chair and walked up to each person, waiting for an answer. "Copy, copy," Santos, Valeria, and I replied in turn. Aleisha chuckled and moved on, satisfied. In June, Santos and her two daughters had crossed the border near El Paso, Texas, where they were arrested and separated under the Trump Administration's zero-tolerance policy. Santos spent the next forty-five days being moved from one detention center to another in Texas, while Valeria and Aleisha were held together in a facility for children in Arizona. "In the shelter," Valeria, who is sixteen, told me, "we had roll call every thirty minutes, and the staff had walkie-talkies." Aleisha had learned to imitate their sign-offs.

Santos and her daughters were released from government custody and reunited two weeks ago, thanks to a federal judge's order and the persistence of the family's immigration attorney. They then resumed the journey that they had begun this spring, when they left Honduras hoping to reach the Washington, D.C., area, where Miguel Calix, Santos's longtime boyfriend and Aleisha's father, lives. On July 17th, when Santos and the girls landed at Ronald Reagan Washington National Airport, Calix was there waiting for them with a bouquet of roses. A small crowd of reporters and well-wishers had accompanied him, in anticipation of the family's reunion, and cameras flashed as the couple and the children all hugged.

For the next few days, the family ran errands in a state of half-stunned relief. Aleisha had left the children's shelter with diarrhea and a dry cough, and she was sleeping fitfully. They drove her to a local medical clinic for a checkup, where she and Valeria also received vaccinations. Afterward, Calix took everyone to buy clothes. "We were starting from scratch," Santos told me. "We needed everything." The family's lawyer, an attorney from El Paso named Linda Corchado, had contacted local volunteers and put out a call for donations. On their first Saturday at home, a mail truck arrived with boxes of gifts. "There were school supplies, utensils, kitchenware, games, and clothes," Santos told me. She had taken photos of the boxes piled high in the driveway. Amazon gift cards were still arriving in the mail every day, with notes written by strangers, welcoming them to the U.S. "When we first got here, it was great," Santos said. "I cooked for everyone, including the landlady and her family. And we were all together."

Immigration laws are dense and inflexible, but the lives they're meant to regulate are inescapably varied and complex. Santos, who is thirty-six years old, lived in Minnesota in the early two-thousands. That's where she met Calix, who is a decade older than she is; he had come to the U.S. from Honduras in 1990 and had since attained U.S. citizenship. The couple planned to get married. But, before they did, Santos was arrested for shoplifting, and then deported to Honduras, in 2009. Since she had overstayed the visa she first used to come to the U.S., the government barred her from returning for ten years. Calix, who is a carpenter, sent money to support her and the children and flew to visit them every few months. After Aleisha was born, Calix and Santos began working with a lawyer to get Aleisha legal status in the U.S., as the daughter of a citizen. But, again, their plans were interrupted. Last fall, Santos took a job as a poll worker in her small town in northern Honduras and reported a case of voter fraud. Men associated with the country's main political party chased her out of town, then tracked her down in the city of San Pedro Sula, where she had fled. She decided to seek asylum in the U.S. "Before I left, we came to an agreement," Santos told me. "I told Miguel that if I got deported back to Honduras, or got turned back along the way, then he'd have to move to Honduras. He agreed, even though he'd be giving up his work in the U.S." Santos has a middle daughter, Rachell, who was born in Minnesota eleven years ago, and is thus a U.S. citizen. There was no reason for her to make the perilous overland journey, and she stayed behind with her grandmother. The plan was for her to come later, by plane, once Santos safely crossed the border. Rachell pleaded with her mother to take her along. "I want to be illegal like you," she'd told Santos, before she left.

Santos and Calix told me their story as we sat together, along with Valeria and Aleisha, on two faux-leather couches in their house's cramped living room. Valeria quietly scrolled through her phone, while Aleisha played with a green stuffed turtle. "We never really talked about what happened," Calix told me, referring to Santos and the girls' time in detention. Calix is trim and quiet, with a short beard and graying hair. He teared up as he spoke, and Santos looked away to try to keep from crying herself. She is tall, with dark, alert eyes. Each family member had suffered, but in a different way; now that their time apart was over, they were reluctant to revisit the pain of what had happened.

"When I saw Miguel at the airport, I didn't feel anything," Santos confessed. "I'd waited so long for that moment. But when it happened, nothing came out. We just looked at each other. It was an ugly feeling." She and Calix told me they'd been fighting a lot since they'd been reunited. "Anything sets it off," Santos said. Calix added, "I'll say to them that I couldn't sleep while they were in detention, that I was so stressed. Wendy will say, 'You were having trouble sleeping? But at least you were in bed at home!' And I understand that." I later learned, from Santos, that Calix had needed emergency abdominal surgery while they were in detention. He went back to work the next day, not wanting to miss a paycheck. "Still, there are times when

I hold him responsible for what we went through," Santos told me. The government agreed to let her pursue her asylum claim, and released her pending

> **Immigration laws are dense and inflexible, but the lives they're meant to regulate are inescapably varied and complex.**

the outcome of her case. She was fitted with an ankle monitor and received strict instructions to stay at home every Friday so that officers from Immigration and Customs Enforcement could confirm that she was living at the address the government had on file.

While the four of us talked, Aleisha bounded around the room, clamoring for attention, and the family laughed. Aleisha prodded Valeria, nestled in her lap, and kept grasping at her hands. She was completely fixated on her older sister. "It's been like this ever since they got out," Santos told me. Aleisha and Valeria slept in the same room while they were in detention, in Arizona. Now that they were home, anytime her sister left the room, Aleisha scurried after her. She would only eat when Valeria did. When she needed to go to the bathroom, she yelled "Tachis"—her version of Francis, Valeria's first name, which she can't yet pronounce—and held out her hand.

Valeria tended to her patiently, but looked exasperated. At one point, she had told Santos that she never wanted to have kids of her own. She has a teen-ager's reserve, and when she speaks there are traces of deeper, more hidden thoughts. "Valeria gave me strength when we were separated," Santos told me. "She never cried on the phone with me, even though I was crying. She said to me, 'Mom, I'll stay strong for you.' When Aleisha was sick, she didn't tell me, because she didn't want me to get upset."

Calix had originally planned for Santos and the girls to stay with his brother, outside Baltimore. But his brother got nervous before they arrived—even though he is in the country legally. ("Since immigration authorities were involved, he didn't want any trouble," Calix told me.) Calix had been renting a room in a small white house, with a modest living room that opens onto the kitchen on the first floor and a cluster of tiny bedrooms upstairs. His landlord, a Dominican nurse, lived there with her husband, and the couple had been looking to rent out one of the other extra bedrooms. After his brother backed out, Calix asked his landlord if he could rent one of the other rooms for the girls.

The house felt claustrophobic. On my first night in town, Aleisha had a fever and cried for hours. The landlord, her husband, and their nephew, who was visiting, were annoyed. "It's gotten complicated here," Santos told me the next morning. The landlord's nephew rarely cleaned up after himself, but the landlord was blaming Santos. She also gave the girls a hard time if they went outside to play, according to Santos. Santos and the girls were spending most of their days in their rooms, with the doors closed. "We watch the news a lot," Valeria told me. Santos said, "The landlady comes home from work around five, and her nephew's been getting home at about one. I get up at four in the morning, with Miguel, and make food for the day. Then I get out of the way. At night, the families eat separately."

On Friday night, I made plans to accompany the family out to dinner at a Mexican restaurant. When I arrived at the house, Santos and her daughters were sitting on the front stoop, eating popsicles. "Miguel's inside fighting with the landlady," Santos told me. He emerged a few minutes later. "I'm paying for my room and for the kids' room, but they keep taking out their frustration on Wendy. She has to clean up. She has to do this and that," he told me. "Once, when Wendy and I were arguing, she told us we were setting a bad example for the children."

We drove to the restaurant, where the mood lightened. Aleisha called out the names of objects on the wall (a horse, a guitar, a sombrero). I sat between Valeria and Calix, who ordered a beer and wanted to talk about American politics. He had theories about Michael Cohen. At work that day, there'd been a discussion of Trump's family-separation policy. A white guy on his construction crew, whom Calix had always liked, asked, "Why are these people coming here? Don't they know there's nothing for them?" Calix couldn't believe his co-worker was so incurious about what Santos and others were fleeing. "People don't even want to bother to educate themselves. They don't care," he said.

A few times during dinner, Aleisha needed to go to the bathroom and nudged Valeria to take her, but she stayed closer to her mother, which tended to happen when they went out, Santos told me. "When we're home, she's back to Valeria," she said. Valeria was taking advantage of the momentary reprieve to send text messages on WhatsApp. When I asked her if she missed her friends in Honduras, she nodded. "I never wanted to come here," she said. She made up excuses to tell her friends at home, first to explain the circumstances of the family's trip to the U.S. and then to account for why she'd been unreachable for the forty-five days she spent in detention. She told me, "I said I got into a fight with my mother, because I was so depressed about having to come here, and that she took my phone away so I couldn't text or send messages."

When we said goodbye in the parking lot later that night, Calix proposed that I swing by the house the next morning to take Santos and the girls out while he was at work. Because it was a Saturday, the landlord and her family would be home, and Santos dreaded the awkwardness. Early the next morning, however, I received a text message from Calix, calling me off. "Wendy and the girls are not at home. Last night, when we got back, the landlord was waiting for us. She told us we had to leave." They relocated to a hotel, while Calix figured out what to do next. "It's one thing after another these days," he said. "We'll be fine. I just have to think."

## Print Citations

**CMS:** Blitzer, Jonathan. "Reunited, an Immigrant Family Tries to Put Their Life Back Together." In *The Reference Shelf: The American Dream,* edited by Annette Calzone, 13-17. Ipswich, MA: H.W. Wilson, 2018.

**MLA:** Blitzer, Jonathan. "Reunited, an Immigrant Family Tries to Put Their Life Back Together." *The Reference Shelf: The American Dream.* Ed. Annette Calzone. Ipswich: H.W. Wilson, 2018. 13-17. Print.

**APA:** Blitzer, J. (2018). Reunited, an immigrant family tries to put their life back together. In Annette Calzone (Ed.), *The reference shelf: The American Dream* (pp. 13-17). Ipswich, MA: H.W. Wilson. (Original work published 2018)

# Six Immigrant Stories That Will Make You Believe in the American Dream Again

By Monte Burke
*Forbes*, October 25, 2016

Thomas Peterffy was born in . . . a Budapest hospital on Sept. 30, 1944. His mother had been moved there because of a Soviet air raid. After the Soviets liberated Hungary from Nazi occupation, Hungary became a satellite state, laboring under a different kind of oppression: communism. Peterffy and his family, descended from nobles, lost everything. . . . As a young man Peterffy dreamed about being free from that prison—in America. . . .

Peterffy landed at John F. Kennedy International Airport in New York City in December 1965. He had no money and spoke no English. He had a single suitcase . . . Peterffy went to Spanish Harlem, where other Hungarian immigrants had formed a small community. . . . He was happy, if not a bit afraid. "It was a big deal to leave home and my culture and my language," he says. "But I believed that in America, I could truly reap what I sowed. . . . This was the land of boundless opportunity."

Indeed it was. He got a job . . . in a surveying firm. When his firm bought a computer, "nobody knew how to program it, so I volunteered to try," he says. He caught on quickly and soon had a job as a programmer for a small Wall Street consulting firm, where he built trading models.

By the late 1970s Peterffy had saved $200,000 and founded a company that pioneered electronic stock trades. . . . In the 1990s he began to concentrate on the sell side of the business, founding Interactive Brokers Group, which has a market cap of $14 billion. Peterffy, 72, is now worth an estimated $12.6 billion.

Thomas Peterffy embodies the American Dream. So does Google founder Sergey Brin ($37.5 billion). And eBay founder Pierre Omidyar ($8.1 billion). And Tesla and SpaceX founder Elon Musk ($11.6 billion). And Rupert Murdoch, George Soros, Jerry Yang, Micky Arison, Patrick Soon-Shiong, Jan Koum, Jeff Skoll, Jorge Perez, Peter Thiel. . . .[They] immigrated to this country, earned U.S. citizenship—and then a spot on the *Forbes* 400.

Precisely 42 slots on the *Forbes* 400 belong to naturalized citizens who immigrated to America. That's 10.5% of the list, a huge overperformance considering that naturalized citizens make up only 6% of the U.S. population. . . . For all the political bombast about immigrants being an economic drain or a security threat, the pace of economic hypersuccess among immigrants is increasing. Go back ten years and the number of immigrants on the *Forbes* 400 was 35. Twenty years ago it was 26 and 30 years ago 20. Not only is the American Dream thriving, as measured by the yardstick of entrepreneurial success, the *Forbes* 400, but it's also never been stronger. The combined net worth of those 42 immigrant fortunes is $248 billion.

According to the Kauffman Foundation, immigrants are nearly twice as likely to start a new business than native-born Americans. The Partnership for a New American Economy, a nonpartisan group formed by *Forbes* 400 members Murdoch and Michael Bloomberg, reports that immigrants started 28% of all new businesses in the U.S. in 2011, employ one out of every ten American workers at privately owned businesses and generate $775 billion in revenue. . . . The National Foundation for American Policy, a nonpartisan research group, says that 44 of the 87 American tech companies valued at $1 billion or more were founded by immigrants. . .

By and large the immigrants of the *Forbes* 400 fall into two baskets. Many, like Peterffy, came here to escape something. Sergey Brin's family left Russia when he was 6 years old because of discrimination against his Jewish family. George Soros survived Nazi-occupied Hungary. Igor Olenicoff's family was forced to leave the U.S.S.R. after World War II because of their tsarist connections.

Others had enough privilege to live anywhere but saw America as the place of greater opportunity. Musk attended private schools in South Africa. Murdoch's father was a knighted Australian newspaper publisher. Omidyar's father was a surgeon.

Rich or poor, America's entrepreneurial mind-set links them all. Americans-by-choice appreciate the opportunity and understand the corollary: that you can't count on anyone giving you a break but instead need to make it yourself. . . .

> **For all the political bombast about immigrants being an ecnomic drain, the pace of hypersuccess among immigrants is increasing.**

Do Won Chang and his wife, Jin Sook, arrived at LAX . . .in 1981[,] . . . the same year martial law was lifted in South Korea. He immediately scoured newspaper job listings [and began working at] a local coffee shop. . . . [H]e tacked on eight hours a day at a gas station and on top of that started a small office-cleaning business. . . .

While pumping gas, Chang noticed that men in the garment business drove nice cars, inspiring him to take a job in a clothing store. Three years later, after he and Jin Sook saved $11,000, they opened a 900-square-foot apparel store called Fashion 21. First-year sales reached $700,000, and the couple began opening a new store every six months, eventually changing the chain's name to Forever 21. They're now worth $3 billion. . .

[S]ays Chang. "I'll always have a grateful heart toward America for the opportunities that it's provided me."

For Shahid Khan, a Pakistani, the logical place to immigrate was the United Kingdom, "but the U.S. was always the promised land for me." In January 1967 Khan landed at JFK . . . [and] the 16-year-old flew to St. Louis . . . and took a bus to

Champaign, to the University of Illinois, where he was enrolled as an undergraduate. He had $500 in his pocket. Khan got a job working as a dishwasher at night after school for $1.20 an hour. "I was overjoyed. You just couldn't get a job like that where I came from," he says. "My immediate thought was, Wow, I can work. I can be my own man. I control my destiny."

Khan eventually got a job as an engineering manager at Flex-N-Gate, an automotive manufacturer. A few years later, with $16,000 in savings and a Small Business Administration loan, he started his own company, which made bumpers for car manufacturers. He eventually bought out his old boss at Flex-N-Gate. His company now has $6.1 billion in revenues and employs around 12,000 people in the U.S.

A plant he's building in Detroit will employ up to 1,000 workers who will be paid $25 an hour. Khan is worth an estimated $6.9 billion. . .

The U.S. educational system has traditionally been a beacon, drawing the smartest . . . young self-starters from across the world. Over the past few decades the billionaire formula has been increasingly simple: Come to America for college, fall in love with the country and the opportunities (and perhaps a future spouse), and stay here after graduation, putting that education to use creating the innovations (and jobs) that yield *Forbes* 400 fortunes.

Romesh Wadhwani falls into that tradition. He attended India's legendary IIT Bombay technical college but in 1969 came to America to pursue a Ph.D. at Carnegie Mellon. He never left, founding Aspect Development, a software company, and Symphony Technology Group, a tech-focused private equity firm, on his way to a $3 billion fortune.

"It would have been virtually impossible for me to have started my own company in India in those days. There was no support for entrepreneurs," says Wadhwani. "There is a freedom in the U.S. to dream big dreams, the freedom to achieve based purely on merit rather than family background or previous wealth or social status."

Chinese-born Andrew Cherng observed a similar meritocracy when he arrived in Baldwin, Kans. in 1966 to attend Baker University on a math scholarship. He'd gone to high school in Japan and found "it was hard for Chinese to blend in with the Japanese." A year later he met an incoming freshman from Burma named Peggy, whom he would later marry. "I didn't have any personal possessions when I came," says Cherng. "My drive came from being poor."

In 1973 Cherng opened a restaurant, the Panda Inn, in California with his father, a master chef who had emigrated to join him. Ten years later he and his wife, Peggy, opened the first Panda Express in a mall in Glendale, Calif. Having earned a doctorate in electrical engineering and worked as an aerospace-software-development engineer, she incorporated systems that have turned it into a 1,900-store, quick-serve food chain, one of the largest in the U.S., with $2.4 billion in revenues. The Cherngs employ 30,000 people and have raised more than $100 million for charity. "In America nothing will stop you but yourself," says Cherng.

Douglas Leone is another *Forbes* 400 member for whom an American education was a turning point. He was in middle school when he left Italy in 1968. His parents envisioned a life for him that included "upward mobility, something that wasn't possible in Europe." He wound up at Cornell and then earned postgraduate degrees from Columbia and MIT. "The American Dream is realized if you take advantage of the opportunity," he says. . . . Leone worked sales jobs for . . . Sun Microsystems and Hewlett-Packard before joining venture capital firm Sequoia Capital in 1988. He became managing partner in 1996. During his tenure Sequoia has invested in Google, YouTube, Zappos, LinkedIn and WhatsApp, and has played a role in the creation of countless jobs. "If I had to bet the over/under on one million jobs created by the companies we've been involved in, I'd bet the over," he says.

Leone is now worth an estimated $2.7 billion. His immigrant experience, he says, has been invaluable. "Being an immigrant provides you with a drive, one that never goes away. I still feel it today," he says. "Failure is not an option. I tell my kids that the only thing I can't give them is desperation. And I apologize to them for that. . . ."

This election cycle's immigrant- and refugee-bashing is a time-honored tradition here, with each wave of newcomers taking its turn in the crosshairs of those who see them as job-stealing criminals. . . . These days the targets are Hispanics and Muslims. "We've gone through these various cycles over the years," says Peter Spiro, a professor at Temple University who specializes in immigration law. "What's meaningful is that we've always come out of them. . . ."

But that dynamic could be challenged. The U.S. has been toughening its visa requirements for skilled workers (the famous H-1B) . . . [and] has had the same visa and quota cap for skilled immigrant workers since 2004, even though demand for the visas has exceeded the mandated allotment.

[T]he government has filled its quota within five days of opening it each year since 2014—at a time when a global economy means that many newly minted college graduates see more opportunity. . . in returning home.

As a result we're increasingly drawing the world's best and brightest, giving them access to our best knowledge—and then kicking them out, against their wishes, to compete with us from their original homeland.

So, what to do? Ask the *Forbes* 400 immigrants, including Peterffy, Khan, Wadhwani and Cherng. . . .[Y]ou'll find agreement on three broad principles.

First, educated and highly motivated immigrants should be encouraged, not discouraged, to come to the U.S. . . . Second, American borders should be more secure when it comes to illegal immigrants. And third, there should be a path to citizenship for illegal immigrants already in the U.S., which includes registering, paying taxes and following the law.

Perhaps this can help create some consensus, one that ensures that the American Dream stays exactly that. How fitting if it proved to be another billion-dollar innovation dreamed up by immigrants.

## Print Citations

**CMS:** Burke, Monte. "6 Immigrant Stories That Will Make You Believe in the American Dream Again." In *The Reference Shelf: The American Dream,* edited by Annette Calzone, 18-22. Ipswich, MA: H.W. Wilson, 2018.

**MLA:** Burke, Monte. "6 Immigrant Stories That Will Make You Believe in the American Dream Again." *The Reference Shelf: The American Dream.* Ed. Annette Calzone. Ipswich: H.W. Wilson, 2018. 18-22. Print.

**APA:** Burke, M. (2018). 6 immigrant stories that will make you believe in the American dream again. In Annette Calzone (Ed.), *The reference shelf: The American Dream* (pp. 18-22). Ipswich, MA: H.W. Wilson. (Original work published 2016)

# The Unique Traits Americans Developed from Decades of Immigration

### By Ana Campoy
### *Quartz*, February 13, 2018

The US Congress is again debating how to permanently welcome Dreamers, the hundreds of thousands of undocumented immigrants who came to the US as children.

A core question for lawmakers will be whether that means significantly downsizing the ideal of America as a country of immigrants: In exchange for letting Dreamers stay, Donald Trump is demanding an end to "chain migration," the family reunification policy that, by the president's own definition, describes how millions of immigrants became Americans.

But that kind of anti-immigrant push is nothing new. In the early 1900s, a backlash against immigrants led to stiff restrictions in 1924. By 1965, Americans were up on immigration again, and the restrictions were replaced with a more open immigration system. US politicians have gone back-and-forth on immigration many times since—even as immigrants have kept coming.

If Donald Trump succeeds in passing his nativist agenda, history suggests Americans will eventually reverse it. As studies in psychology, sociology and political science show, immigration is deeply imprinted on US culture, from the way Americans smile to the environments that make them feel most at home.

## The Way Americans Smile

Trump has spotlighted—and emboldened—a sector of American society that feels threatened by immigrants. White Americans, in particular, are anxious about becoming a minority, and are therefore feeling less fond of diversity, research shows.

But there are multiple reasons to believe those are not the attitudes that will prevail. Immigration has defined the US and its citizens from the very start—down to how often and why they smile.

Smiling, and showing emotions in general, is more common in countries that are historically diverse than in homogenous places, say researchers from Niedenthal Emotions Lab, at the University of Wisconsin, Madison. Individuals in diverse societies have to rely on emotional expression to navigate the panoply of foreign cultures, social norms, and languages they came across during the course of everyday life.

Among nine countries studied by the researchers, the US had the highest share of people who see smiles as a way to be friendly or bond with others—more than 80%. In more homogenous countries, such as Japan, people are less likely than Americans to crack a smile to show friendliness, and more likely to do it to assert their superiority.

## The Way Americans Think

Immigration is also embedded into Americans' psychology. "All Americans, that is, all non-Indian Americans, have left an old world behind," wrote the late Bruce Mazlish, a Massachusetts Institute of Technology professor known for applying the lens of psychoanalysis to history. That separation, along with the tensions and contradictions it generated, shaped who they became in their new world, he continued in a 1990 book of essays.

Here's how Mazlish describes those early drivers of the American way:

> The need to return to the ideal and reverse a declension; the need to experience a rebirth; the need for sons to stand free of their parents, especially fathers; and the need to repudiate the traditions and values of the old civilization of Europe. From being an English colonist now emerges an American.

Some of them are still tangible today, for example, in Americans' spirit of independence and individuality. The notion of a new beginning still shapes how Americans—and foreigners—see the US. It's visible in enduring ideals such as the American dream or in the real rags-to-riches stories of foreign entrepreneurs.

## The Way Americans Hear

Immigrants to the US—and their descendants—don't have the millenary myths or ethnic homogeneity that binds the citizens of their countries of origin. What they have in common is the immigrant experience, and the civic values enshrined in the Constitution. That's why the melting pot concept continues to have currency, even among immigration hawks, who say it's not *immigration* that's the problem, but illegal immigration.

"Even people quite opposed to increased immigration nonetheless go out of their way to make it very clear they are very staunch backers of legal immigration," says Daniel Hopkins, a political scientist at University of Pennsylvania who researches attitudes towards immigrants. (Ultra- immigration hardliner and Republican politician Tom Tancredo, for example, launched his presidential bid in 2007 on the premise that "the great tradition of the melting pot in America" was not working due to illegal immigration.)

> **If Donald Trump succeeds in passing his nativist agenda, history suggests Americans will eventually reverse it.**

Hopkins's studies also suggest that Americans are less hostile to immigrants who demonstrate their willingness to "melt" into the proverbial pot. In fact, in one of his experiments, subjects who watched clips of immigrants speaking with varying degrees of English fluency were more supportive of the ones with broken accents.

"The native-born Americans hear that effort and think of that immigrant in the tradition of generations and generations of immigrants coming to the US and seeking a better life," he says.

## The American Welcome

American attitudes on immigration are not solely rooted on the longstanding ideal of the US as the land of opportunity. They are also in large part based on everyday interactions with today's immigrants. And research suggests that when Americans live with immigrants, they warm up to them. "The immigrants' experience gets woven into the lives of the entire region," says Stanford professor Tomás Jiménez.

A recent study he co-authored gives an idea to what extent. It sought to determine the impact of local policies designed to welcome immigrants—or repel them—on the broader community. Jiménez and his colleagues asked white and Latino residents in New Mexico and Arizona to randomly consider two sets of policies, one welcoming to immigrants, the other hostile. They then tallied how the two sets of policies made participants feel—angry, happy, or sad—and whether they left them feeling at home in their state or wanting to move elsewhere.

It's no surprise that the welcoming policies elicited positive feelings among immigrants and gave them a greater sense of belonging. But those policies also had a positive effect on people who were born in the US—with the exception of white conservatives. (Hostile measures made white conservatives feel more positive, and at home.) This is what the researchers concluded:

> These findings suggest that debates about the polarizing effects of immigration policies by racial group are misplaced. With a majority of whites nationally identifying as either liberal or moderate, welcoming immigration policies have direct and spillover effects that can further national unity.

In other words, a community that welcomes immigrants makes most non-immigrants feel more welcome, too.

## Print Citations

**CMS:** Campoy, Ana. "The Unique Traits Americans Developed from Decades of Immigration." In *The Reference Shelf: The American Dream,* edited by Annette Calzone, 23-26. Ipswich, MA: H.W. Wilson, 2018.

**MLA:** Campoy, Ana. "The Unique Traits Americans Developed from Decades of Immigration." *The Reference Shelf: The American Dream.* Ed. Annette Calzone. Ipswich: H.W. Wilson, 2018. 23-26. Print.

**APA:** Campoy, A. (2018). The unique traits Americans developed from decades of immigration. In Annette Calzone (Ed.), *The reference shelf: The American Dream* (pp. 23-26). Ipswich, MA: H.W. Wilson. (Original work published 2018)

# The Decades-Long Campaign to Cut Legal Immigration

By Jonathan Blitzer

*The New Yorker,* August 8, 2017

Last week, when Donald Trump publicly endorsed the *RAISE* Act, a bill that would drastically curb legal immigration to the United States, he did what immigration hard-liners had waited more than two decades for a President to do. The bill, whose acronym is short for Reforming American Immigration for Strong Employment, was introduced in February by Senators Tom Cotton and David Perdue, both Republicans, but it hadn't attracted much attention until Trump took up its mantle. "This legislation demonstrates our compassion for struggling American families who deserve an immigration system that puts their needs first," Trump said at a White House press conference. "Our people, our citizens, and our workers," he went on, have struggled while "competing for jobs against brand-new arrivals."

While Trump made combating illegal immigration a cornerstone of his Presidential campaign, he also pledged to limit legal immigration. It's this side of the issue that's addressed in the *RAISE* Act. If it becomes law, it would cut the number of legal permanent residents allowed into the country each year from a million to five hundred thousand, mainly by limiting the number of foreign family members that current residents are allowed to sponsor. Family unity has been one of the core principles of the U.S.'s immigration system since the nineteen-sixties—anyone with citizenship or a green card is allowed to sponsor family members—but the *RAISE* Act would cap the number of green cards allocated to family sponsors, and eliminate family sponsorship beyond spouses and minor children. The bill would also implement a point system that would rank applicants seeking to come to the U.S. for work—about a hundred and fifty thousand such people come to the U.S. every year—and give an advantage to immigrants who already speak English.

Proposals to cut legal immigration aren't exactly new in Washington. When comprehensive immigration-reform bills were debated in 2006, 2007, and 2013, conservative lawmakers briefly and unsuccessfully pushed to include similar measures. But the last time a plan to cut legal immigration received the kind of attention currently enjoyed by the *RAISE* Act was 1996. Then, as now, Republicans controlled both chambers of Congress. Lamar Smith, a congressman from Texas, was the primary force behind a set of sweeping reforms to both legal and illegal immigration. But his effort to cut legal immigration failed: a majority of Senate Republicans, including Mitch McConnell, and a third of House Republicans voted against it. Congress then passed an elaborate system of penalties and enforcement measures for illegal immigration that became the Illegal Immigration Reform and Immigrant Responsibility Act of 1996. That bill, which was signed by President Bill Clinton, laid the groundwork for the system of mass deportation that's in effect today.

Questioning legal immigration hasn't been an exclusively conservative position, however. "Today the Democratic Party is seen as being completely in the pro-immigration column, and the Republican Party as being in the anti-immigrant column," Muzaffar Chishti, an immigration expert at the Migration Policy Institute, told me. "But it wasn't always that way." In the nineteen-eighties and nineties, Democrats, channelling the concerns of organized labor, considered low-skilled immigrants a threat to wages and jobs. Their rhetoric then sounded like Trump's last week. But as Democrats began

> **Questioning legal immigration hasn't been an exclusively conservative position.**

to feel that their political future depended on a growing population of Hispanic voters, their message changed. The early two-thousands were littered with mea culpas and about-faces from prominent Democrats who, just years before, had taken strong stances against immigration. In 2006, for example, the Democratic Senate Majority Leader, Harry Reid, who in 1993 introduced a bill to eliminate birthright citizenship, issued a dramatic apology on the Senate floor. Then, in 2010, he excoriated Republicans for advancing a birthright citizenship measure of their own.

And while mainstream members of the Republican Party were once more aligned with pro-business conservatives, who were sanguine about the economic advantages of immigrant workers, a more strident wing—epitomized by Smith and Jeff Sessions, who left the Senate to become the Attorney General—began pushing a more general anti-immigrant line that, decades later, has won out in the Trump Administration. "Now that the Administration has increased immigration enforcement, it's turning to legal immigration," Chishti told me. "This is completely out of the Sessions playbook. It did not begin with Trump." This playbook is literal: in 2015, Sessions and his staff produced a twenty-three-page document called "Immigration Handbook for the New Republican Majority." It anatomized how the federal government was failing to enforce immigration laws, and how immigration was causing wages to stagnate and unemployment to persist. Many of these ideas were included in the Republican Party's platform last year, which, for the first time in the Party's history, called for an explicit reduction in legal immigration. For anti-immigration stalwarts, it was Sessions's involvement in Trump's campaign that won their support. "Sessions was Trump's Good Housekeeping seal of approval," Mark Krikorian, the head of the influential anti-immigration think tank Center for Immigration Studies, told me. "Sure, Trump is not a real conservative and he's a little bit unusual, but he's got Sessions."

It's unlikely that the *RAISE* Act will become law—even today, many Republicans in Congress would likely vote against it. (Some, like Lindsey Graham, have already publicly criticized it.) But in Trump, nativist activists and lawmakers finally have someone in the White House who speaks their language. "For the first time ever, a President has sought a reduction in legal immigration," Chishti told me. "Even when Congress has been hostile to immigration, the President has always stood on the other side of the issue. This is from Wilson to Truman; it was true of Kennedy and Johnson and Reagan, all the way to George W. Bush and Obama. There have been no exceptions—until now."

## Print Citations

**CMS:** Blitzer, Jonathan. "The Decades-Long Campaign to Cut Legal Immigration." In *The Reference Shelf: The American Dream,* edited by Annette Calzone, 27-29. Ipswich, MA: H.W. Wilson, 2018.

**MLA:** Blitzer, Jonathan. "The Decades-Long Campaign to Cut Legal Immigration." *The Reference Shelf: The American Dream.* Ed. Annette Calzone. Ipswich: H.W. Wilson, 2018. 27-29. Print.

**APA:** Blitzer, J. (2018). The decades-long campaign to cut legal immigration. In Annette Calzone (Ed.), *The reference shelf: The American Dream* (pp. 27-29). Ipswich, MA: H.W. Wilson. (Original work published 2017)

# Places in the US That Took in More Immigrants in the 19th Century Still Benefit Economically from It

By Dan Kopf
*Quartz*, June 3, 2017

In the late 19th century, immigrants came to the United States in droves. The absolute number of immigrants in the country rose from less than 2.5 million in 1850 to more than 13.5 million in 1910. That boosted immigrants as a share of the population to 15%, from 10%, over the period.

That group of immigrants was similar in many ways to those entering the US today. Most did not speak English, followed different religious practices than the natives, and were fleeing politically or economically treacherous situations. The majority were unskilled laborers, though a small number were highly educated.

According to a recently published study, the immigrants of the late 19th and early 20th century have had a remarkably positive and long-lasting impact on the places where they settled. The research by economists from Harvard, Yale, and the London School of Economics found that, today, US counties that received more immigrants from 1860 to 1920 have "significantly higher incomes, less poverty, less unemployment, more urbanization and higher educational attainment." For example, they estimate that a 5% increase in the share of immigrants to a county during this period led to a 20% boost to average incomes in 2000.

It's not just that immigrants went to the most economically promising places, but that the presence of immigrants led to increased economic growth. The researchers demonstrate this through a cleverly identified natural experiment.

At the time, immigrants to the US travelled to their new homes in the interior of the country primarily by railroad. If a town was connected to the railroad, immigrants were more likely to settle there. And although migration was high throughout this period, there were certain years when events, usually political or weather related, made even more people want to leave their home country and come to the US. If a county was first connected to the railroad during one of these boom years, it received an unusually high number of immigrants. Places that were first connected in more subdued years received fewer immigrants. Whether a county was connected to the railroad during a boom year was pure happenstance, the researchers establish, making this a perfect natural experiment to understand the long-term effects of immigration.

The researchers believe the late 19th and early 20th century immigrants stimulated growth because they were complementary to the needs of local economies at that time. Low-skilled newcomers were supplied labor for industrialization, and higher-skilled arrivals helped spur innovations in agriculture and manufacturing.

> **The late 19th and early 20th century immigrants stimulated growth because they were complementary to the needs of local economies at that time.**

The data also show that the long-term benefits of immigration did not come at short-term cost to the economy as a whole. More immigrants almost immediately led to more vibrant economies. The study has little to say, however, on the short-term impact of immigrants on the wages of natives, a debate that continues to rage today in the US and elsewhere.

Of course, the current economic and political circumstances are quite different from the late 19th century, but there are enough similarities to suggest that the benefits of immigration would hold true in the 21st century and beyond. Even if increasing immigration reduces some local workers' wages in the short-term, the evidence suggests that descendants of these workers would end up better off.

## Print Citations

**CMS:** Kopf, Dan. "Places in the US That Took in More Immigrants in the 19th Century Still Benefit Economically from It." In *The Reference Shelf: The American Dream*, edited by Annette Calzone, 30-31. Ipswich, MA: H.W. Wilson, 2018.

**MLA:** Kopf, Dan. "Places in the US That Took in More Immigrants in the 19th Century Still Benefit Economically from It." *The Reference Shelf: The American Dream*. Ed. Annette Calzone. Ipswich: H.W. Wilson, 2018.30-31. Print.

**APA:** Kopf, D. (2018). Places in the US that took in more immigrants in the 19th century still benefit economically from it. In Annette Calzone (Ed.), *The reference shelf: The American Dream* (pp. 30-31). Ipswich, MA: H.W. Wilson. (Original work published 2017)

# 2
# Mobility and Equality

"We Are the 99%," at an Occupy Wall Street protest. The affluent "1 percent" collectively own most of the nation's wealth, making it increasingly difficult to climb the economic ladder and achieve the American Dream.

# The Great American Success Story

The American dream is a national ethos—popularized in the 1930s but with older philosophical roots—saying that any person who works hard enough or has sufficient talent can achieve a better life in America. Those who embrace the American dream as real believe that talent and hard work allow one to achieve economic mobility, meaning the ability to rise up the economic ladder, and that the United States provides a uniquely favorable environment for achieving success. In reality, the United States does not offer an easier path to success than many other economically advanced nations. This is partly due to what is called "wealth inequality," a situation in which the nation's wealthy control an outsized share of the nation's resources and use this wealth to maintain the status quo. Wealth and income inequality are among the nation's chief economic problems and have been a subject of intense academic research and public debate for much of the last half-century.

## The Roots of Success

Many of America's richest individuals are born into a wealthy family and are, by birth, members of what is now typically called the "1 percent"—the one percent of Americans who collectively possess 40 percent of the nation's wealth (more wealth than the bottom 90 percent of Americans combined). While there is nothing inherently wrong with achieving success in part because of one's family wealth, being born into the wealthy class provides an incontrovertible advantage for financial success. Americans assign less value to this kind of success and see it as less representative of the American dream.

Speaking about this issue in an article for the *Guardian*, reporter Maia Szalavitz wrote,

> Americans reflexively connect hard work with deservingness. The American dream promises that if we work hard enough we will be rewarded, and that those who have wealth deserve to have it. We don't think much about why a hedge-fund manager would "deserve" exponentially more than a doctor, scientist or teacher—or whether the measure of a person's "worth" should be only economic.[1]

While Americans celebrate success based on innovative talent and skill, such success is rare and becoming rarer. Numerous economic studies have confirmed that if a person begins life with capital for investment in their future, it is a better determinant of success than talent, work ethic, or intelligence. Even in proverbial rags-to-riches narratives, it is becoming increasingly clear that chance and circumstance are far more impactful than generally believed.

A 2018 paper by Italian physicists Alessandro Pluchino and Andrea Rapisarda and economist A.E. Biondo presents a study of wealth in Western societies that compares various determinants of success. As the authors write,

> The largely dominant meritocratic paradigm of highly competitive Western cultures, is rooted on the belief that success is due mainly, if not exclusively, to personal qualities such as talent, intelligence, skills, smartness, efforts, willfulness, hard work or risk taking.

However, the authors argue that the distribution of wealth does not confirm this belief. Given the fact that intelligence, skill, creativity, and talent should be more or less evenly distributed, success, too, should be evenly distributed. The fact that it is not means that the distribution of wealth cannot be explained by the possession of those characteristics. What makes the difference? It's partially down to luck. The authors' calculations indicate that the world's smartest, most creative, or most talented people will almost never also be the most successful.[2] If the researchers are correct, it may be fitting that a large amount of money or assets is also called a "fortune."

## A Problem of Movement

When examining success, one of the metrics commonly used is to look at what economists call "mobility," which can be described as the potential for a person to move up or down the economic ladder. The American dream of prosperity had its origins in an age when America was a chaotic and rapidly growing market driven by voracious expansionism. With an economy innovated by immigrant labor and entrepreneurism, America's melting pot became among the most creative and productive in the world during the industrial revolution, eventually catapulting the nation to global economic dominance. This fostered the impression that the nation was unique in its ability to encourage innovation and success.

While Americans have proudly clung to this vision of the nation's exceptionalism, success is more difficult to achieve for most Americans than in much of the rest of what is now called Western civilization. A Brookings International report from 2002 indicated that a child born poor in America is more likely to remain poor than in most of Europe. Whereas in the 1950s each generation of Americans had a good chance of earning more than their parents, in the twenty-first century, fewer and fewer Americans exceed their parent's level of wealth. In fact, an increasing percentage of Americans earn less comparatively, adjusting for changes in the cost of living.

Part of the reason for America's declining economic mobility is wage stagnation. Wages for most American workers have remained virtually unchanged for the past 40 years, while increases in the cost of living and rising inflation rates mean that actual purchasing power has declined.[3] Had American wages grown in conjunction with economic productivity, an American earning $40,000 in the 2018 market should be making closer to $60,000.[4] Not only are fewer Americans advancing in wealth, but the present-day wealth of many Americans is decreasing within their own lifetime. Studies indicate that income inequality in the United States is more acute in the 2010s than it has been since the Great Depression.

## Inequality

Given that it has become more difficult for Americans to increase their personal wealth, and given too that the share of wealth controlled by the elite class continues to grow, some have suggested that the American dream is dead or dying, or at least that it is under threat. This broad field of economic problems creates what has been called "economic insecurity," an emotional reaction to the uncertainty that America's troubled economic system engenders in many Americans.

A host of studies has established that Americans are uniquely depressed among the residents of the world's developed nations. In early 2018, Gallup reported that "subjective well-being," a person's internal sense of happiness or satisfaction, is declining around the country. Researchers found that Americans demonstrate dissatisfaction with their standard of living, increased rates of depression, and a decline in feeling supported by family and community.[5] While economic anxiety is at the heart of American depression, studies also show that wealthy countries are, in general, more depressed than poor countries.[6]

The contradictory character of America might, in fact, be a function of America's ideology. The downside of believing that all one needs to succeed is talent, skill, intelligence, or hard work means that those who fail to improve their situation face the implication that they must be lacking in one or more of these categories. The realization that merit alone rarely leads to success, and that even the most hardworking and talented struggle to overcome economic challenges, might provide a sense of perspective on one's own perceived failings.

## Works Used

Florida, Richard. "The Unhappy States of America." *Citylab*. Atlantic Monthly Group. Mar 20, 2018. Retrieved from https://www.citylab.com/life/2018/03/the-unhappy-states-of-america/555800/.

Gould, Elise. "The State of American Wages 2017." *EPI*. Economic Policy Institute. Mar 1, 2018. Retrieved from https://www.epi.org/publication/the-state-of-american-wages-2017-wages-have-finally-recovered-from-the-blow-of-the-great-recession-but-are-still-growing-too-slowly-and-unequally/.

Gunn, Dwyer. "How to Give American Workers Fair Wages." *PSmag*. Pacific Standard. Mar 9, 2018. Retrieved from https://psmag.com/economics/how-to-give-american-workers-fair-wages.

Pappas, Stephanie. "US and France More Depressed Than Poor Countries." *Lifescience*. Purch Media. Jul 25, 2011. Retrieved from https://www.livescience.com/15225-global-depression-poor-rich-countries.html.

Solman, Paul. "Analysis: If You're Rich, You're More Lucky Than Smart: And There's Math to Prove It." *PBS News Hour*. Nine Network. May 15, 2018. Retrieved from https://www.pbs.org/newshour/economy/making-sense/

analysis-if-youre-rich-youre-more-lucky-than-smart-and-theres-math-to-prove-it.

Szalavitz, Maia. "What's Behind Rich People Pretending to Be Self-Made?" *The Guardian*. The Guardian News and Media. Jan 29, 2018. Retrieved from https://www.theguardian.com/us-news/2018/jan/29/rich-people-wealth-america.

## Notes

1. Szalavitz, "What's Behind Rich People Pretending to Be Self-Made?"
2. Solman, "Analysis: If You're Rich, You're More Lucky Than Smart: And There's Math to Prove It."
3. Gunn, "How to Give American Workers Fair Wages."
4. Gould, "The State of American Wages 2017."
5. Florida, "The Unhappy States of America."
6. Pappas, "US and France More Depressed Than Poor Countries."

# Economic Inequality: It's Far Worse Than You Think

By Nicholas Fitz
*Scientific American*, March 31, 2015

## The Great Divide between Our Beliefs, Our Ideals, and Reality

In a candid conversation with Frank Rich last fall, Chris Rock said, "Oh, people don't even know. If poor people knew how rich rich people are, there would be riots in the streets." The findings of three studies, published over the last several years in *Perspectives on Psychological Science*, suggest that Rock is right. We have no idea how unequal our society has become.

In their 2011 paper, Michael Norton and Dan Ariely analyzed beliefs about wealth inequality. They asked more than 5,000 Americans to guess the percentage of wealth (i.e., savings, property, stocks, etc., minus debts) owned by each fifth of the population. Next, they asked people to construct their ideal distributions. Imagine a pizza of all the wealth in the United States. What percentage of that pizza belongs to the top 20% of Americans? How big of a slice does the bottom 40% have? In an ideal world, how much should they have?

The average American believes that the richest fifth own 59% of the wealth and that the bottom 40% own 9%. The reality is strikingly different. The top 20% of US households own more than 84% of the wealth, and the bottom 40% combine for a paltry 0.3%. The Walton family, for example, has more wealth than 42% of American families combined.

We don't want to live like this. In our ideal distribution, the top quintile owns 32% and the bottom two quintiles own 25%. As the journalist Chrystia Freeland put it, "Americans actually live in Russia, although they think they live in Sweden. And they would like to live on a kibbutz." Norton and Ariely found a surprising level of consensus: everyone—even Republicans and the wealthy—wants a more equal distribution of wealth than the status quo.

This all might ring a bell. An infographic video of the study went viral and has been watched more than 16 million times. In a study published last year, Norton and Sorapop Kiatpongsan used a similar approach to assess perceptions of income inequality. They asked about 55,000 people from 40 countries to estimate how much corporate CEOs and unskilled workers earned. Then they asked people

> **The United States is now the most unequal of Western nations.**

how much CEOs and workers *should* earn. The median American estimated that the CEO-to-worker    pay-ratio was 30-to-1, and that ideally, it'd be 7-to-1. The reality? 354-to-1. Fifty years ago, it was 20-to-1. Again, the patterns were the same for all subgroups, regardless of age, education, political affiliation, or opinion on inequality and pay. "In sum," the researchers concluded, "respondents underestimate actual pay gaps, and their ideal pay gaps are even further from reality than those underestimates."

These two studies imply that our apathy about inequality is due to rose-colored misperceptions. To be fair, though, we do know that *something* is up. After all, President Obama called economic inequality "the defining challenge of our time." But while Americans acknowledge that the gap between the rich and poor has widened over the last decade, very few see it as a serious issue. Just five percent of Americans think that inequality is a major problem in need of attention. While the occupy movement may have a tangible legacy, Americans aren't rioting in the streets.

One likely reason for this is identified by a third study, published earlier this year by Shai Davidai and Thomas Gilovich that suggests that our indifference lies in a distinctly American cultural optimism. At the core of the American Dream is the belief that anyone who works hard can move up economically regardless of his or her social circumstances. Davidai and Gilovich wanted to know whether people had a realistic sense of economic mobility.

The researchers found Americans overestimate the amount of upward social mobility that exists in society. They asked some 3,000 people to guess the chance that someone born to a family in the poorest 20% ends up as an adult in the richer quintiles. Sure enough, people think that moving up is significantly more likely than it is in reality. Interestingly, poorer and politically conservative participants thought that there is more mobility than richer and liberal participants.

According to Pew Research, most Americans believe the economic system unfairly favors the wealthy, but 60% believe that most people can make it if they're willing to work hard. Senator Marco Rubio says that America has "never been a nation of haves and have-nots. We are a nation of haves and soon-to-haves, of people who have made it and people who will make it." Sure, we love a good rags-to-riches story, but perhaps we tolerate such inequality because we think these stories happen more than they actually do.

We may not want to believe it, but the United States is now the most unequal of all Western nations. To make matters worse, America has considerably less social mobility than Canada and Europe.

As the sociologists Stephen McNamee and Robert Miller Jr. point out in their book, "The Meritocracy Myth," Americans widely believe that success is due to individual talent and effort. Ironically, when the term "meritocracy" was first used by Michael Young (in his 1958 book "The Rise of the Meritocracy") it was meant to criticize a society ruled by the talent elite. "It is good sense to appoint individual people to jobs on their merit," wrote Young in a 2001 essay for the *Guardian*. "It is the opposite when those who are judged to have merit of a particular kind harden into a new social class without room in it for others." The creator of the phrase wishes we would stop using it because it underwrites the myth that those who have money and power must deserve it (and the more sinister belief that the less fortunate don't deserve better).

By overemphasizing individual mobility, we ignore important social determinants of success like family inheritance, social connections, and structural discrimination. The three papers in *Perspectives on Psychological Science* indicate not only that economic inequality is much worse than we think, but also that social mobility is less than you'd imagine. Our unique brand of optimism prevents us from making any real changes.

George Carlin joked that, "the reason they call it the American Dream is because you have to be asleep to believe it." How do we wake up?

## Print Citations

**CMS:** Fitz, Nicholas. "Economic Inequality: It's Far Worse Than You Think." In *The Reference Shelf: The American Dream*, edited by Annette Calzone, 39-41. Ipswich, MA: H.W. Wilson, 2018.

**MLA:** Fitz, Nicholas. "Economic Inequality: It's Far Worse Than You Think." *The Reference Shelf: The American Dream*. Ed. Annette Calzone. Ipswich: H.W. Wilson, 2018. 39-41. Print.

**APA:** Fitz, Nicholas. Economic inequality: It's far worse than you think. In Annette Calzone (Ed.), *The reference shelf: The American Dream* (pp. 39-41). Ipswich, MA: H.W. Wilson. (Original work published 2017)

# The Cost of the American Dream

*The Economist,* September 8, 2017

Paul Ryan, the Speaker of the House of Representatives, recently tweeted that, "[i] n our country, the condition of your birth does not determine the outcome of your life. This is what makes America so great." The idea that every American newborn has an equal opportunity to enjoy the good life is false. But it isn't just the Speaker who radically underestimates the importance of the lottery of birth—his is a popular view country-wide. And that is one of the reasons why debates about tax in America are so heated.

Richer parents can afford to send their children to better schools and colleges and can offer financial support for housing and other expenses. For these and a host of other reasons, where and to whom you are born is a significant determinant of life outcomes, especially in America. Miles Corak of the University of Ottawa reports that it is possible to predict nearly 50% of the variation in wages of sons in the United States by looking at the wages of their fathers a generation before. That compares to less than 20% in relatively egalitarian countries like Finland, Norway and Denmark. In America, more than half of sons born to fathers in the top decile of incomes fall no further than the eighth decile themselves, while only about half of those born to bottom decile father rise higher than the third decile.

Taking a broader perspective, the role of birth luck looks even larger. Branko Milanovic, an economist, suggests that two thirds of global income distribution can be explained simply by looking at where people live. According to World Bank data, the average monthly consumption of the richest 10% of Tanzanians was $173 in 2012. In America, the lowest decile sees an average income of $226. That there is simply no overlap in decile consumption between the two countries is not because Tanzanians are all layabouts who made poor life choices, but because they live in a poor country. Being born in America is worth so much because it means you've won the between-country birth lottery.

That is not what most Americans believe, however. Pew surveys suggest that 57% of Americans disagree with the idea that "success in life is pretty much determined by forces outside of our control." That's considerably above the global average, and compares to 31% disagreeing in Germany, for example.

Mr. Ryan's colleagues are particularly likely to share his opinions on American meritocracy. Benjamin Newman, a political scientist at the University of Connecticut and his colleagues looked at the results of surveys and found that rich people in America were more inclined to believe in meritocracy while poor people emphasised the role of luck. The median net worth of a member of Congress was $1,029,505 in 2013. That

> **Where and to whom you are born is a significant determinant of life outcomes, especially in America.**

compares to a national household median net worth of $56,355 according to the Centre for Responsive Politics.

There are straightforward policy fixes that can reduce unequal opportunity at birth. One of them is taxation. Evelyne Huber, a political scientist at the University of North Carolina and her colleagues looked at the income share of the top 1% across rich countries from 1960 to 2012. They found that raising the top tax rate reduces the share of the 1%. Increasing taxes reduces inequality and lower inequality is itself associated with lower inheritance of the inequality that remains.

But that is not the direction that either Congress or the White House is heading. On September 6th, President Donald Trump announced via Twitter: "Will be going to North Dakota today to discuss tax reform and tax cuts. We are the highest taxed nation in the world—that will change."

In fact, amongst the OECD club of rich countries, America's tax revenues are 26.4% of GDP—the fifth lowest. That compares to an OECD average of 34.3% and above 40% in many countries with low inheritance of inequality including Sweden and Denmark. But until more lawmakers in Washington, DC accept that the considerable majority of their income is due to where, when and to whom they were born, the idea that taxes are "unfairly" high will remain prevalent. And that will help perpetuate the country's yawning inequality of opportunity.

## Print Citations

**CMS:** "The Cost of the American Dream." In *The Reference Shelf: The American Dream,* edited by Annette Calzone, 42-43. Ipswich, MA: H.W. Wilson, 2018.

**MLA:** "The Cost of the American Dream." *The Reference Shelf: The American Dream.* Ed. Annette Calzone. Ipswich: H.W. Wilson, 2018. 42-43. Print.

**APA:** The Economist. (2018). The cost of the American dream. In Annette Calzone (Ed.), *The reference shelf: The American Dream* (pp. 42-43). Ipswich, MA: H.W. Wilson. (Original work published 2017)

# Inequality and the American Dream

By Ben Casselman
*FiveThirtyEight*, December 8, 2016

Decades of rising income inequality and slowing economic growth have eroded a pillar of the American dream: the hope that each generation will do better than the one that came before, according to new research released Thursday.

If the findings hold up, they have profound economic, social and even political implications. The decline in what economists call "mobility"—how easy it is to move up the income ladder over a lifetime or across generations—has been especially stark in the Rust Belt states that helped propel Donald Trump to victory in last month's presidential election.

In 1970, according to the research, conducted by Stanford economist Raj Chetty and several co-authors, roughly nine out of every 10 American 30-year-olds earned more than their parents did at the same age, after adjusting for inflation. In 2014, only half of 30-year-olds could say the same.[1] The slowdown in mobility shows up in all 50 states and is true across the income spectrum. The biggest declines were among the children of middle-class families.

The researchers identify two main drivers of the drop in mobility. First, economic growth has slowed in recent decades. That means the economic pie is growing more slowly than it used to, which makes it harder for each generation to surpass the previous one—there is less new income to go around. Second, income inequality has risen, which means that fewer people are benefiting from any new income being generated. Chetty and his colleagues estimate that inequality is more than twice as important as slowing growth, accounting for more than 70 percent of the decline in mobility.

Their research comes out the same week as a separate study by French economist Thomas Piketty and others that found that the bottom half of American adults by income today earn no more in pre-tax income than the bottom half of American adults did in the 1970s.

"There really is a dramatic change in what's going on in the income distribution in the U.S.," said Nathaniel Hendren, an economist at Harvard and another of the latest paper's authors. "The rungs of the ladder are growing further apart, so the difference in outcomes in being born to a rich family versus being born to a poor family is getting greater."

Chetty and Hendren's research, which is based on an analysis of tax records and Census Bureau data, hasn't yet been subjected to peer review, and it relies on a novel methodology for linking parents' and children's incomes that will doubtless face scrutiny from other economists. But Chetty is widely respected, and his work has been cited by both liberals and conservatives. The paper tries to address some of the most frequent conservative criticisms of related work, including that directed at Piketty.

The research is the latest in a series of papers from Chetty, Hendren and their co-authors looking at patterns in economic mobility in the U.S. The researchers have previously studied what is known as relative mobility, which measures how much the economic pecking order is reshuffled from one generation to the next— how likely it is, for example, that someone born into the poorest 20 percent of households will rise to the richest 20 percent. They found that relative mobility varies significantly from one part of the country to another but overall hasn't changed much over time.

In their new paper, the researchers tried to measure a different concept, absolute mobility: How likely is it that someone will earn more than his or her parents did? Unlike the relatively flat line of relative mobility, the trend for absolute mobility points clearly downward. Nearly all Americans born in the 1940s, regardless of income, could expect to out-earn their parents in adulthood (or live in households that did). But mobility fell sharply over the next 20 years: Just 70 percent of Americans born in 1955 out-earned their parents at age 30, and only about 60 percent of those born in 1960 did so. The decline has slowed since then, but it hasn't stopped: Among Americans born in the early 1980s, barely half have managed to surpass their parents' earnings.

> **The economic pie is growing more slowly than it used to, which makes it harder for each generation to surpass the previous one—there is less new income to go around.**

Notably, the one break from the downward trend came among Americans born in the late 1960s and early 1970s, who entered their prime working years during the economic boom of the late 1990s. That suggests that economic growth—and especially the kind of broad-based prosperity that was a hallmark of that boom—could help improve mobility. The researchers tested that theory by analyzing what the mobility would have looked like had economic growth remained as high as it was in the middle of the 20th century. Sure enough, mobility would have improved: 62 percent of Americans born in 1980 would have out-earned their parents instead of the 50 percent seen in the real world.

But inequality was a much bigger driver. The researchers analyzed a scenario in which growth followed its real-world path, but that growth was distributed more equally. In that scenario, the rate of mobility would rise to 80 percent, wiping out more than two-thirds of the 40-year decline.

Ultimately, Hendren said, restoring mobility will require both. "You need growth, and you need it to be broad-based," Hendren said.

The paper's findings are consistent with other evidence of declining American prosperity, such as the stagnation in household income and the shrinking of the middle class. In the past, some economists, particularly on the right, have challenged such claims. They argue, for example, that researchers often focus too much on measures of income that ignore the effects of taxes and government programs that help the poor. And they say government figures often overstate inflation in part by failing to account fully for improving quality and technological developments—houses and cars are bigger and better-made today than they were in the 1970s, but those improvements don't show up in inflation statistics. That makes the stagnation in household income—and related problems, such as declining mobility—look worse than it really is, these critics argue.

The new paper, however, finds that the decline in mobility looks more or less the same even when looking at after-tax income, using alternative measures of inflation or making other adjustments such as accounting for the shrinking size of the typical U.S. family. Those factors influence the levels of mobility—exactly how likely it is for children to out-earn their parents—but they don't change the overall downward trend.

Hendren said he and his colleagues were surprised at how consistent—and stark—the results were, cutting across regions and income groups. "This is something that is just [affecting] kids of all backgrounds," Hendren said.

1. These figures refer to household income. The authors also looked at individual income—comparing sons to their fathers, for example—and other measures. All show the same general trend.

## Print Citations

**CMS:** Casselman, Ben. "Inequality and the American Dream." In *The Reference Shelf: The American Dream*, edited by Annette Calzone, 44-46. Ipswich, MA: H.W. Wilson, 2018.

**MLA:** Casselman, Ben. "Inequality and the American Dream." *The Reference Shelf: The American Dream*. Ed. Annette Calzone. Ipswich: H.W. Wilson, 2018. 44-46. Print.

**APA:** Casselman, B. (2018). Inequality and the American dream. In Annette Calzone (Ed.), *The reference shelf: The American Dream* (pp. 44-46). Ipswich, MA: H.W. Wilson. (Original work published 2016)

# The American Dream, Quantified at Last

By David Leonhardt
*The New York Times*, December 8, 2016

The phrase "American dream" was invented during the Great Depression. It comes from a popular 1931 book by the historian James Truslow Adams, who defined it as "that dream of a land in which life should be better and richer and fuller for everyone."

In the decades that followed, the dream became a reality. Thanks to rapid, widely shared economic growth, nearly all children grew up to achieve the most basic definition of a better life—earning more money and enjoying higher living standards than their parents had.

These days, people are arguably more worried about the American dream than at any point since the Depression. But there has been no real measure of it, despite all of the data available. No one has known how many Americans are more affluent than their parents were—and how the number has changed.

It's a thorny research question, because it requires tracking individual families over time rather than (as most economic statistics do) taking one-time snapshots of the country.

The beginnings of a breakthrough came several years ago, when a team of economists led by Raj Chetty received access to millions of tax records that stretched over decades. The records were anonymous and came with strict privacy rules, but nonetheless allowed for the linking of generations.

The resulting research is among the most eye-opening economics work in recent years. You've probably heard some of the findings even if you don't realize it. They have shown that the odds of escaping poverty vary widely by region, for instance, an insight that has influenced federal housing policy.

After the research began appearing, I mentioned to Chetty, a Stanford professor, and his colleagues that I thought they had a chance to do something no one yet had: create an index of the American dream. It took them months of work, using old Census data to estimate long-ago decades, but they have done it. They've constructed a data set that shows the percentage of American children who earn more money—and less money—than their parents earned at the same age.

The index is deeply alarming. It's a portrait of an economy that disappoints a huge number of people who have heard that they live in a country where life gets better, only to experience something quite different.

Their frustration helps explain not only this year's disturbing presidential campaign but also Americans' growing distrust of nearly every major societal institution, including the federal government, corporate America, labor unions, the news media and organized religion.

Yet the data also helps point the way to some promising solutions.

It begins with children who were born in 1940, less than a decade after the publication of Adams's book, *The Epic of America*. The researchers went into the project assuming that most of these children had earned more than their parents—but were surprised to learn that nearly all of them had, said David Grusky, one of the researchers, also of Stanford. About 92 percent of 1940 babies had higher pretax inflation-adjusted household earnings at age 30 than their parents had at the same age. (The results were similar at older ages and for post-tax earnings.)

> **The solution has to involve some combination of faster economic growth and more widely shared growth.**

The few 1940 children who earned less than their parents were also, for the most part, doing just fine. They were generally earning less because they had grown up rich—children of top corporate executives, say, who became, or married, doctors, lawyers or professors.

Achieving the American dream was a virtual guarantee for this generation, regardless of whether people went to college, got divorced or suffered a layoff. Why? Because they spent their prime working years in an economy with two wonderful features. It was growing rapidly, and the bounty from its growth flowed to the rich, the middle class and the poor alike.

Not even the oldest baby boomers, born in the late 1940s and early 1950s, would be quite so lucky. Economic growth began to slow as they were entering the job market in the 1970s, thanks in part to the energy crises. Still, more than three-quarters of these early Baby Boomers would ultimately make more than their parents. . .

In the 1980s, economic inequality began to rise, a result of globalization, technological change, government policies favoring the well-off and a slowdown in educational attainment and the work force's skill level. Together, these forces pinched the incomes of the middle class and the poor. The tech boom of the 1990s helped—slowing the decline of the American dream—but only temporarily.

For babies born in 1980—today's 36-year-olds—the index of the American dream has fallen to 50 percent: Only half of them make as much money as their parents did. In the industrial Midwestern states that effectively elected Donald Trump, the share was once higher than the national average. Now, it is a few percentage points lower. There, going backward is the norm.

Psychology research has shown that people's happiness is heavily influenced by their relative station in life. And it's hard to imagine a more salient comparison than to a person's own parents, particularly at this time of year, when families gather for rituals that have been repeated for decades. "You're going home for the holidays and you compare your standard of living to your parents," Grusky, a sociologist, says. "It's one of the few ties you have over the course of your entire life. Friends come and go. Parents are a constant."

How, then, can the country revive Adams's dream of a "better and richer and fuller" life for everyone? The solution has to involve some combination of faster economic growth and more widely shared growth.

The bad news is that lifting G.D.P. growth is terribly difficult. Trump has promised to do so, but offered few specifics. If anything, he favors some of the same policies (deregulation and tax cuts) that have failed in recent decades.

The better news—potentially—is that lifting growth is the less important half of the equation, notes Nathaniel Hendren of Harvard, another of the researchers: The rise of inequality has damaged the American dream more than the growth slowdown.

One way to think about inequality's role is to remember that the American economy is far larger and more productive than in 1980, even if it isn't growing as rapidly. Per-capita G.D.P. is almost twice as high now. By itself, that increase should allow most children to live better than their parents.

They don't, however, because the fruits of growth have gone disproportionately to the affluent.

The researchers ran a clever simulation recreating the last several decades with the same G.D.P. growth but without the post-1970 rise in inequality. When they did, the share of 1980 babies who grew up to out-earn their parents jumped to 80 percent, from 50 percent. The rise was considerably smaller (to 62 percent) in the simulation that kept inequality constant but imagined that growth returned to its old, faster path.

"We need to have more equal growth if we want to revive the American dream," Chetty says.

Given today's high-tech, globalized economy, the single best step would be to help more middle- and low-income children acquire the skills that lead to good-paying jobs. Notably, most college graduates still earn more than their parents did, other data show—yes, even after taking into account student debt.

But education is not the only answer. Incomes have also stagnated because of the rise of corporate power and the weakening of labor unions, leading profits to rise at the expense of wages. The decline of two-parent families plays a role, too. And tax policy has not done enough to push back against these forces: The middle class, not the affluent, deserves a tax cut.

The painful irony of 2016 is that nostalgia and anger over the fading American dream helped elect a president who may put the dream even further out of reach for many people—taking away their health insurance, supporting ineffective school vouchers and showering government largess on the rich. Every one of those issues will be worth a fight.

If the American dream could survive the Depression, and then thrive in a way few people imagined, it can survive our current troubles.

## Print Citations

**CMS:** Leonhardt, David. "The American Dream, Quantified at Last." In *The Reference Shelf: The American Dream*, edited by Annette Calzone, 47-50. Ipswich, MA: H.W. Wilson, 2018.

**MLA:** Leonhardt, David. "The American Dream, Quantified at Last." *The Reference Shelf: The American Dream*. Ed. Annette Calzone. Ipswich: H.W. Wilson, 2018. 47-50. Print.

**APA:** Leonhardt, D. (2018). The American dream, quantified at last. In Annette Calzone (Ed.), *The reference shelf: The American Dream* (pp. 47-50). Ipswich, MA: H.W. Wilson. (Original work published 2016)

# Is Owning a Home Still Essential to the American Dream?

By Nicholas Padiak
*The Chicago Tribune*, June 7, 2017

Ah, the American Dream: You work hard, get a good job, start a family, buy a house and then, when you're done with that house, you buy a bigger one. You accumulate wealth in your home and then pass that wealth on to your children, who will be better off than you.

That's the American Dream, right?

Right?

"I guess if your definition of the American Dream hasn't changed since, like, the '50s," said freelance camera operator Dan Niederkorn, 24, of the Chicago suburb of Montgomery.

Niederkorn, a member of the millennial generation, currently lives with his parents but said he plans to be a renter for life and never buy a home. He craves the ability to pack up and go, he said, and doesn't want to be saddled with a home loan, property taxes or homeowners associations fees. And though this may put him in the minority—an *Apartment List* survey of about 24,000 renters nationwide released in May found that 80 percent of millennial renters want to buy a house or condo sometime in the future—it does raise some interesting questions about the American Dream and the place of homeownership within it.

## History of Homeownership

To really examine what we know of as the American Dream, it helps to start by looking at the history of homeownership in the United States.

"The U.S. wasn't always a nation of homeowners," said Brian McCabe, assistant sociology professor at Georgetown University and author of the book *No Place Like Home: Wealth, Community, and the Politics of Homeownership.*

"The homeownership rate really starts to climb after the Second World War," McCabe said. "So it's in the 1950s and the 1960s that we go from being a country of 45 percent (homeownership) to a country of well over 60 percent."

There are many reasons for this shift, McCabe said, citing the rise of the suburbs, the postwar baby boom, low interest rates offered to soldiers returning from the war and the evolution of mortgages into the relatively low-down-payment, extended-loan-period products we commonly see today.

"This is really the creation of the federal government," Mc-Cabe said. "We thought what it meant to be a good citizen was very caught up in what it meant to own property in the United States."

> An Apartment List survey found that 80 percent of millennial renters want to buy a house or condo sometime in the future.

Of course, as with most things political, the government didn't act entirely on its own, according to Eugene White, professor of economics at Rutgers University and co-editor of the book *Housing and Mortgage Markets in Historical Perspective*.

"As we know, in taxes or anything else, there's a great deal of lobbying which goes on in Congress," White said. "And the housing industry has been very successful in getting breaks ... which induce people to buy houses."

The breaks White referred to are some of the biggest incentives toward home-ownership today, according to Greg Nagel, managing broker of Ask Nagel Realty in Chicago's West Town community area.

Homeownership, said Nagel, "represents probably the most risk-free investment opportunity to build wealth due to the tax advantages," such as the mortgage interest and property tax deductions. "It's very powerful," he said.

## Effects of Crisis Deeply Felt

But as was made painfully clear during the housing crisis of 2007-08, real estate investments aren't always a sure thing. And this knowledge may loom large for an entire generation of Americans.

"A lot of millennials' conceptions about homeownership are shaped by the experiences they went through during their formative years," said Phoenix-based attorney James Goodnow, shareholder and director at Fennemore Craig P.C. and co-author of the book *Motivating Millennials*.

"When the housing bubble burst in 2008, millennials saw their parents, their grandparents and their friends lose their homes, have them given back to the bank," Goodnow said. "And I think that caused millennials to have some skepticism of the benefits of homeownership in the way that previous generations just did not."

Of course, some young people didn't just watch their friends and families get overtaken by the housing crisis. Some experienced it firsthand.

"I bought a condo pretty close after college in 2008, which in hindsight, I realize, what a bad time," said sales engineer Julia Napolitano, 32, of Milwaukee.

"I went into it, really, with this idea of, 'I want to establish myself. I want to build my career, I want to build a home,'" Napolitano said. "And in my mind, growing up in a single-family home my entire life with my parents, that was their marker. That was what they really instilled in me."

But then, "The market changed and with it so did my opinion of homeownership," Napolitano said.

After buying her condo for $159,000 and living in it for a few years, Napolitano moved into a rental unit and leased her home to renters. Finally, in 2016, she sold her condo for $104,000.

"I needed to get away from it," she said, noting that even when the unit was rented, she was either barely breaking even or taking a financial loss every month. Plus, she said, life as a landlord just didn't suit her.

Jeremy Smolik, 37, of Chicago's Forest Glen neighborhood, had a similar experience with a unit he purchased in Rogers Park for $195,000 in 2007.

"I figured, you know, this is great," Smolik, a technology salesman, said. "I can have a property in Chicago that I could own for 30 years and make some money on it and pass it along to my kids or sell it off and use the assets towards a larger home eventually."

But by the time Smolik got his unit appraised in 2012, he found that it was worth only $78,000. After living in the home for seven years, Smolik moved out and began leasing the unit to renters.

"Constantly fixing up stuff and finding leaks and repairing things, it's just, it's been a headache," he said.

These experiences aren't unique to just a few young people here and there, according to Richard Green, director and chair of University of Southern California's Lusk Center for Real Estate.

"If you bought a house in 2003, 2004, 2005, OK, you probably at least have equity in your house now," Green said. "But you haven't substantially increased your equity. In generations past ... the equity was just there to buy the second house, and people don't have that now. And I think that's probably the most profound lingering impact of the crisis."

## Dark Cloud of Debt

Another issue that can't be overlooked: "Millennials are dealing with crushing student debt," attorney and author Goodnow said.

Indeed, the Federal Reserve Bank of New York reported that by the end of 2016, the national student debt had reached $1.31 trillion, and that 2015 graduates with loans left school with an average of about $34,000 in student debt.

"Student debt is making my generation more anxious," said Adam Smiley Poswolsky, millennial workplace expert and author of *The Quarter-Life Breakthrough: Invent Your Own Path, Find Meaningful Work, and Build a Life That Matters.*

"A lot of the traditional signposts of success were simply not available to my generation," Poswolsky said, pointing to the student debt crisis, the difficult housing market and the recession that many young people walked into. "So (millennials are) much more focused on purpose in their life in the present and less focused on that white picket fence or that thing in the past that used to be kind of a signal of, oh, you've achieved the American Dream."

And even if young people do want to buy a home, said White, the Rutgers economics professor, "getting a mortgage is no longer as easy as it used to be. The terms are much more difficult. The banks are compensating for mistakes they made."

Add to this the tough market, with soaring home prices and housing inventory 9 percent lower than it was a year ago, according to the National Association of Realtors.

Throw in the hassles of maintaining a property you own.

Sprinkle in a dash of the freedom that comes with renting.

And when it's all mixed together, you could be forgiven for wondering whether purchasing a home is even worth it—and whether that cornerstone of the American Dream is losing its luster.

Well ... not so fast.

## Pathway to Wealth

"There aren't a lot of opportunities to build wealth outside of homeownership," said McCabe, "and we rely on our wealth, this wealth that we've built, for retirement, for weathering health emergencies, maybe sending our kids to college. And homeownership still remains the best way to build wealth."

For the most part, according to McCabe, people recognize this, and many—even millennials—are not entirely put off by homeownership.

Yes, some young people shun the suburbs with their dreaded white picket fences. "If I move to a suburb, most suburbs," said millennial workplace expert Poswolsky, "am I going to be around people who share my similar values? No."

But McCabe, the assistant sociology professor, sees this as more of a delay than anything else.

"For a lot of millennials, they'll spend some time in the city in their 20s before they move out to the suburbs," he said. "Maybe the draw of buying a home kicks in a little bit later. They might not be thinking about building wealth and starting families as young."

So is homeownership still a cornerstone of the American Dream? Depends on whom you ask.

Ask economics professor White, and he'll say: "The American Dream is not about homeownership, but it's about upward mobility. Some people may never buy a house, and yet their status and income will rise. So it's really a matter of choice. It's not the be-all and end-all."

Ask attorney Goodnow, and he'll say: "I think homeownership is part of the American Dream for millennials, but it's no longer the cornerstone of that dream."

Ask former homeowner Napolitano, and she'll say: "I think it's going to be more about fulfilling the needs of a lifestyle and a desire for a particular type of lifestyle than just a desire to have a house."

In the end, perhaps the most important person to ask is yourself.

## Print Citations

**CMS:** Padiak, Nicholas. "Is Owning a Home Still Essential to the American Dream?" In *The Reference Shelf: The American Dream*, edited by Annette Calzone, 51-55. Ipswich, MA: H.W. Wilson, 2018.

**MLA:** Padiak, Nicholas. "Is Owning a Home Still Essential to the American Dream?" *The Reference Shelf: The American Dream*. Ed. Annette Calzone. Ipswich: H.W. Wilson, 2018. 51-55. Print.

**APA:** Padiak, N. (2018). Is owning a home still essential to the American dream? In Annette Calzone (Ed.), *The reference shelf: The American Dream* (pp. 51-55). Ipswich, MA: H.W. Wilson. (Original work published 2017)

# 3
# Race and the American Dream

A 50th-anniversary ceremony at the Lincoln Memorial commemorating the watershed March on Washington, where Martin Luther King, Jr., famously declared: "I have a dream." Despite desegregation and affirmative action, nonwhite individuals still face challenges to achieving the American Dream.

# Dreaming in Color

Race is a difficult and perennially controversial topic in the United States. Recent events highlighting police brutality and inspiring the Black Lives Matter protest movement have brought race to the forefront of the national conversation, and an increasing number of Americans believe that America needs to adopt new strategies to address racial hatred and tension. According to a Pew Research report from October 2017, most Americans (61 percent) now believe that America needs to make more changes to achieve racial equality, while 35 percent believe that America has done enough to achieve this goal. As recently as 2014, however, a slight majority of Americans (49 to 46 percent) believed that America had already made the necessary changes to reach this goal.[1]

Among those who study race relations and sociology, there is near total agreement that the United States still has a serious problem with racism and has not made the changes necessary to achieve racial equality. One of the manifestations of race in the United States includes the fact that nonwhite individuals face unique challenges that make it more difficult for minority men and women to climb the economic ladder or to achieve wealth.

## The Perception of Equity

Yale psychologists conducted a study in 2017 looking at American attitudes about wealth, race, and the progress of the United States in addressing the racial wealth gap, which can be defined as the gap in wealth between black and white Americans connected to racial discrimination. The researchers asked respondents to estimate how much an average black family earned for every $100 earned by a white family and asked them to estimate how much wealth an average black family controlled by every $100 controlled by an average white family. Respondents recognized that there would be a discrepancy between the two and most estimated that black families would earn between $80-$90 for every $100 earned by an average white family, and would command $70-$80 in wealth for every $100 in wealth owned by an average white family. However, these estimates are far more optimistic than the reality, in which the average black family earns only $57 for every $100, and controls just $5.04 for every $100 owned by an average white family.

The results surprised even the authors of the study, many of whom found that they too overestimated the degree to which black families had approached parity in America. One of the study's authors, Jennifer Richeson, told the *New York Times*, "It seems that we've convinced ourselves—and by 'we' I mean Americans write large—that racial discrimination is a thing of the past. We're literally overcome it, so to speak, despite blatant evidence to the contrary."[2]

Research suggests that Americans are highly motivated to believe that the United States is a "fair" and "equitable" society and demonstrate a tendency to misinterpret or reinterpret available information to better match with this view of their country. However, this tendency may ultimately slow the process of addressing racial inequality, as skepticism regarding the need to address racial disparities translates directly into whether or not Americans are willing to support affirmative action policies, or school desegregation policies, or to believe that further efforts are needed to address disparities in hiring or mortgage lending policies.

The reality for black and other minority Americans looking to advance is that there are persistent structural challenges at every level. For instance, a meta-analysis of 24 separate studies of hiring practices found that white applicants for jobs were called back for interviews 36 percent more than black Americans and 24 percent more than Hispanic/Latino Americans over the past 25 years. Studies show further that broader economic changes are not to blame. Whether the economy is in a boom or bust period, and whether or not employment rates go up or down, black Americans have twice the unemployment rate of white Americans across the board.[3]

## The Past Catches Up

Home ownership is an important factor in the generational acquisition of wealth. In 2017, around 64 percent of white Americans own homes or other property, while only around 40 percent of black families own homes.[4] The disparity in home ownership is important because, while home ownership is not sufficient to guarantee economic advancement, studies indicate that home ownership has a generational impact on economic well-being. Children of parents who own homes tend to achieve higher earnings and higher educational levels and are far more likely to own homes or property at some point in their lives.

Further, parents who own homes can leverage their properties to support their children's needs and growth, while home inheritance can also provide the opportunity to reallocate assets and invest in other factors that influence a person's financial success. Even when black families or individuals manage to purchase homes, the impact of segregation and prejudice means that black families more often own property in marginalized neighborhoods with more pronounced fluctuation in property values, thus limiting the beneficial financial impact of home ownership over the longer term.[5] This coupled with ongoing prejudice in lending practices creates a cycle that limits generational wealth within black families.

Factors influencing success and wealth like homeownership provide one example of how the nation's racial past continues to influence the outcomes of nonwhite Americans. When black Americans were all slaves, and thus entirely prohibited from owning property or accruing personal wealth, white families were already generating and accruing a wealth of benefits that continue to influence the outcomes for white men and women in America. White males in particular benefit from what has been called "white privilege," described in a 1997 essay by social scientist Peggy McIntosh, who popularized the term, as an 'invisible package of unearned assets."[6]

In her article "White Privilege and Male Privilege," McIntosh lists 46 examples of benefits that white Americans experience. These range from realizations like no. 1 "I can, if I wish, arranged to be in the company of people of my race most of the time," to serious economic and political reflections like no. 38, "I can think over many options, social, political, imaginative, or professional, without asking whether a person of my race would be accepted or allowed to do what I want to do," to the often underestimated realities of living in an at-times racist society, no. 20, "I did not have to educate our children to be aware of systemic racism for their own daily physical protection," to more subtle issues, like no. 46 "I can choose blemish cover or bandages in 'flesh' color and have them more or less match my skin."[7]

Many white Americans are skeptical about "white privilege" and this likely reflects generational guilt and the high motivation to view American society as fair and balanced. A Pew Research report from 2017 found that a majority of white people (54 percent) feel they get little or no advantage from their race. By contrast, 92 percent of black people and 65 percent of Latino/Hispanic respondents believed that white people benefit from their race in ways that other races do not. The difference in opinion reflects an underlying world view as well, with a full 72 percent of Republicans/conservatives believing that white people receive no benefit from race.[8] Despite this skepticism, there is little doubt that being white in the United States provides a distinct advantage, though not sufficient to guarantee success. White individuals also face serious challenges in the effort to gain success and amass wealth, but racial prejudice and systemic racial prejudice constitute an additional barrier marginalizing America's racial minorities to a higher degree.

While black Americans, in many ways, remain America's most socioeconomically disadvantaged group, black Americans are not the only group economically marginalized in America. Native Americas, for instance, face generational income and investment inequality that continues to affect the outcome for native children and adults. More than one-fourth of Native Americans live in poverty and factors such as governmental mismanagement and exploitation are significant factors perpetuating the cycle of poverty.[9] Caught between preserving their traditional culture and pursuing the mainstream goals of the American dreams (amassing wealth), Native Americans face many barriers—racial, governmental, and societal—to achieving success as well as existing in a culture in which success itself is incommensurate with preserving aspects of their cultural legacy and history. Even more so than black or Latino Americans, racism and the challenges faced by Native Americans are ignored by the majority of Americans. For instance, it is not widely known, but Native Americans are more likely to be killed by police than any other demographic in America, and yet racial violence against Native Americans is rarely covered in the media.[10]

## What Makes Race

For many white Americans, believing in white privilege, or in that the society that they embrace has institutional inequalities that limit the capability of others to advance, may be interpreted as somehow diminishing or delegitimizing their own value and worth. This is similar to how wealthy Americans who have inherited part or most of their wealth demonstrate a distinct tendency to downplay the importance of inheritance and to overestimate the importance of their personal qualities in generating their personal wealth and success. For these wealthy Americans, embracing that their wealth and success is a factor of their being born wealthy, rather than of their personal qualities, puts them at odds with the mainstream view of the American dream, or of America as a land where success is based on merit, and not birthright. It is likely that Americans failure to recognize the deep impact of race is a function of this same capacity for self-delusion as a mechanism to protect one's sense of self-worth. By ignoring or reinterpreting the wealth of data demonstrating the impact of race on well-being, such a person can continue to believe in America as a fair society that rewards actual worth, rather than one in which power and advantage are more important than skill.

## Works Used

Badger, Emily. "Whites Have Huge Wealth Edge Over Blacks (but Don't Know It)." *The New York Times*. The New York Times, Co. Sep 18, 2017. Retrieved from https://www.nytimes.com/interactive/2017/09/18/upshot/black-white-wealth-gap-perceptions.html.

Bouie, Jamelle. "The Wealth Gap Between Whites and Blacks Is Widening." *Slate*. Atlantic Monthly Group. Sep 17, 2017. Retrieved from http://www.slate.com/articles/news_and_politics/politics/2017/09/the_wealth_gap_between_whites_and_blacks_is_widening.html.

Cortright, Joe. "How Housing Intensifies the Racial Wealth Gap." *Citylab*. Atlantic Monthly Group. Sep 22, 2017. Retrieved from https://www.citylab.com/equity/2017/09/how-housing-intensifies-the-racial-wealth-gap/540879/.

Krogstad, Jens Manuel. "One-in-Four Native Americans and Alaska Native Are Living in Poverty. *Pew Research*. Pew Research Center. Jun 13, 2014. Retrieved from http://www.pewresearch.org/fact-tank/2014/06/13/1-in-4-native-americans-and-alaska-natives-are-living-in-poverty/.

Massie, Victoria M. "Native Americans Like Renee Davis Are Ignored When Police Brutality Is Viewed as Black and White." *Vox*. Vox Media. Oct 25, 2016. Retrieved from https://www.vox.com/identities/2016/10/25/13403290/renee-davis-police-violence-native-american.

McIntosh, Peggy. "White Privilege and Male Privilege: A Personal Account of Coming to See Correspondences Through Work in Women's Studies (1988). *Collegeart*. College Art Association of America, Inc. Retrieved from http://www.collegeart.org/pdf/diversity/white-privilege-and-male-privilege.pdf.

Oliphant, Baxter. "Views about Whether Whites Benefit from Societal Advantages Split Sharply along Racial and Partisan Lines." *Pew Research*. Pew Research Center. Sep 28, 2017. Retrieved from http://www.pewresearch.org/fact-tank/2017/09/28/views-about-whether-whites-benefit-from-societal-advantages-split-sharply-along-racial-and-partisan-lines/.

"The Partisan Divide on Political Views Grows Even Wider." *Pew Research*. Pew Research Center. Oct 5, 2017. Retrieved from http://www.people-press.org/2017/10/05/4-race-immigration-and-discrimination/.

Rothman, Joshua. "The Origins of 'Priviledge'." *The New Yorker*. Condé Nast. May 12, 2014. Retrieved from https://www.newyorker.com/books/page-turner/the-origins-of-privilege.

Singletary, Michelle. "Black Homeownership Is as Low as It Was When Housing Discrimination Was Legal." *The Washington Post*. The Washington Post Co. Apr 5, 2018. Retrieved from https://www.washingtonpost.com/news/get-there/wp/2018/04/05/black-homeownership-is-as-low-as-it-was-when-housing-discrimination-was-legal/?utm_term=.4044198321ce.

## Notes

1. "The Partisan Divide on Political Views Grows Even Wider," *Pew Research*.
2. Badger, "Whites Have Huge Wealth Edge Over Blacks (but Don't Know It)."
3. Bouie, "The Wealth Gap Between Whites and Blacks Is Widening."
4. Singletary, "Black Homeownership Is as Low as It Was When Housing Discrimination Was Legal."
5. Cortright, "How Housing Intensifies the Racial Wealth Gap."
6. Rothman, "The Origins Of 'Privilege'."
7. McIntosh, "White Privilege and Male Privilege."
8. Oliphant, "Views about Whether Whites Benefit from Societal Advantages Split Sharply along Racial and Partisan Lines."
9. Krogstad, "One-in-Four Native Americans and Alaska Natives Are Living in Poverty."
10. Massie, "Native Americans Like Renee Davis Are Ignored When Police Brutality Is Viewed as Black and White."

# My Immigrant Family Achieved the American Dream: Then I Started to Question It

By Amanda Machado
*Vox*, January 9, 2017

In summer 2007, I returned home from my freshman year at Brown University to the new house my family had just bought in Florida. It had a two-car garage. It had a pool. I was on track to becoming an Ivy League graduate, with opportunities no one else in my family had ever experienced. I stood in the middle of this house and burst into tears. I thought: *We've made it.*

That moment encapsulated what I had always thought of the "American dream." My parents had come to this country from Mexico and Ecuador more than 30 years before, seeking better opportunities for themselves. They worked and saved for years to ensure my two brothers and I could receive a good education and a solid financial foundation as adults. Though I can't remember them explaining the American dream to me explicitly, the messaging I had received by growing up in the United States made me know that coming home from my first semester at a prestigious university to a new house meant we had achieved it.

And yet, now six years out of college and nearly 10 years past that moment, I've begun questioning things I hadn't before: Why did I "make it" while so many others haven't? Was this conventional version of making it what I actually wanted? I've begun to realize that our society's definition of making it comes with its own set of limitations and does not necessarily guarantee all that I originally assumed came with the American dream package.

I interviewed several friends from immigrant backgrounds who had also reflected on these questions after achieving the traditional definition of success in the United States. Looking back, there were several things we misunderstood about the American dream. Here are a few:

## The American Dream Isn't the Result of Hard Work: It's the Result of Hard Work, Luck, and Opportunity

Looking back, I can't discount the sacrifices my family made to get where we are today. But I also can't discount specific moments we had working in our favor. One example: my second-grade teacher, Ms. Weiland. A few months into the year, Ms.

> **The United States doesn't lack people trying. What it lacks is an equal playing field of opportunity.**

Weiland informed my parents about our school's gifted program. Students tracked into this program in elementary school would usually end up in honors and Advanced Placement classes in high school—classes necessary for gaining admission into prestigious colleges.

My parents, unfamiliar with our education system, didn't understand any of this. But Ms. Weiland went out of her way to explain it to them. She also persuaded school administrators to test me for entrance into the program, and with her support, I eventually earned a spot.

It's not an exaggeration to say that Ms. Weiland's persistence ultimately influenced my acceptance into Brown University. No matter how hard I worked or what grades I received, without gifted placement I could never have reached the academic classes necessary for an Ivy League school. Without that first opportunity given to me by Ms. Weiland, my entire educational trajectory would have changed.

The philosopher Seneca said, "Luck is what happens when preparation meets opportunity." But in the United States, too often people work hard every day, and yet never receive the opportunities that I did—an opportunity as simple as a teacher advocating on their behalf. Statistically, students of color remain consistently undiscovered by teachers who often, intentionally or not, choose mostly white, high-income students to enter advanced or "gifted" programs, regardless of their qualifications. Upon entering college, I met several students from across the country who also remained stuck within their education system until a teacher helped them find a way out.

Research has proved that these inconsistencies in opportunity exist in almost every aspect of American life. Your race can determine whether you interact with police, whether you are allowed to buy a house, and even whether your doctor believes you are really in pain. Your gender can determine whether you receive funding for your startup or whether your attempts at professional networking are effective. Your "foreign-sounding" name can determine whether someone considers you qualified for a job. Your family's income can determine the quality of your public school or your odds that your entrepreneurial project succeeds.

These opportunities make a difference. They have created a society where most every American is working hard and yet only a small segment are actually moving forward. Knowing all this, I am no longer naive enough to believe the American dream is possible for everyone who attempts it. The United States doesn't lack people trying. What it lacks is an equal playing field of opportunity.

## Accomplishing the American Dream Can Be Socially Alienating

Throughout my life, my family and I knew this uncomfortable truth: To better our future, we would have to enter spaces that felt culturally and racially unfamiliar to us. When I was 4 years old, my parents moved our family to a predominantly white part of town, so I could attend the county's best public schools. I was often one of the only students of color in my gifted and honors programs. This trend continued in college and afterward: As an English major, I was often the only person of color in my literature and creative writing classes. As a teacher, I was often one of few teachers of color at my school or in my teacher training programs.

While attending Brown, a student of color once told me: "Our education is really just a part of our gradual ascension into whiteness." At the time I didn't want to believe him, but I came to understand what he meant: Often, the unexpected price for academic success is cultural abandonment.

In a piece for the *New York Times*, Vicki Madden described how education can create this "tug of war in [your] soul":

> To stay four years and graduate, students have to come to terms with the unspoken transaction: exchanging your old world for a new world, one that doesn't seem to value where you came from. … I was keen to exchange my Western hardscrabble life for the chance to be a New York City middle-class museum-goer. I've paid a price in estrangement from my own people, but I was willing. Not every 18-year-old will make that same choice, especially when race is factored in as well as class.

So many times throughout my life, I've come home from classes, sleepovers, dinner parties, and happy hours feeling the heaviness of this exchange. I've had to Google cultural symbols I hadn't understood in these conversations (What is "*Harper's*"? What is "après-ski"?). At the same time, I remember using academia jargon my family couldn't understand either. At a Christmas party, a friend called me out for using "those big Ivy League words" in a conversation. My parents had trouble understanding how independent my lifestyle had become and kept remarking on how much I had changed. Studying abroad, moving across the country for internships, living alone far away from family after graduating—these were not choices my Latin American parents had seen many women make.

An official from Brown told the *Boston Globe* that similar dynamics existed with many first-generation college students she worked with: "Often, [these students] come to college thinking that they want to return home to their communities. But an Ivy League education puts them in a different place—their language is different, their appearance is different, and they don't fit in at home anymore, either."

A Haitian-American friend of mine from college agreed: "After going to college, interacting with family members becomes a conflicted zone. Now you're the Ivy League cousin who speaks a certain way, and does things others don't understand. It changes the dynamic in your family entirely."

A Latina friend of mine from Oakland felt this when she got accepted to the University of Southern California. She was the first person from her to family to leave home to attend college, and her conservative extended family criticized her for leaving home before marriage.

"One night they sat me down, told me my conduct was shameful and was staining the reputation of the family," she told me, "My family thought a woman leaving home had more to do with her promiscuity than her desire for an education. They told me, 'You're just going to Los Angeles so you can have the freedom to be with whatever guy you want.' When I think about what was most hard about college, it wasn't the academics. It was dealing with my family's disapproval of my life."

We don't acknowledge that too often, achievement in the United States means this gradual isolation from the people we love most. By simply striving toward American success, many feel forced to make to make that choice.

## The American Dream Makes Us Focus Single-Mindedly on Wealth and Prestige

When I spoke to an Asian-American friend from college, he told me, "In the Asian New Jersey community I grew up in, I was surrounded by parents and friends whose mentality was to get high SAT scores, go to a top college, and major in medicine, law, or investment banking. No one thought outside these rigid tracks." When he entered Brown, he followed these expectations by starting as a premed, then switching his major to economics.

This pattern is common in the Ivy League: Studies show that Ivy League graduates gravitate toward jobs with high salaries or prestige to justify the work and money we put into obtaining an elite degree. As a child of immigrants, there's even more pressure to believe this is the only choice.

Of course, financial considerations are necessary for survival in our society. And it's healthy to consider wealth and prestige when making life decisions, particularly for those who come from backgrounds with less privilege. But to what extent has this concern become an unhealthy obsession? For those who have the privilege of living a life based on a different set of values, to what extent has the American dream mindset limited our idea of success?

The *Harvard Business Review* reported that over time, people from past generations have begun to redefine success. As they got older, factors like "family happiness," "relationships," "balancing life and work," and "community service" became more important than job titles and salaries. The report quoted a man in his 50s who said he used to define success as "becoming a highly paid CEO." Now he defines it as "striking a balance between work and family and giving back to society."

While I spent high school and college focusing on achieving an Ivy League degree, and a prestigious job title afterward, I didn't think about how other values mattered in my own notions of success. But after I took a "gap year" at 24 to travel, I realized that the way I'd defined the American dream was incomplete: It was not only about getting an education and a good job but also thinking about how my career choices contributed to my overall well-being. And it was about gaining experiences aside from my career, like travel. It was about making room for things like creativity, spirituality, and adventure when making important decisions in my life.

Courtney E. Martin addressed this in her TED talk called "The New Better Off," where she said: "The biggest danger is not failing to achieve the American dream. The biggest danger is achieving a dream that you don't actually believe in."

Those realizations ultimately led me to pursue my current work as a travel writer. Whenever I have the privilege to do so, I attempt what Martin calls "the harder, more interesting thing": to "compose a life where what you do every single day, the people you give your best love and ingenuity and energy to, aligns as closely as possible with what you believe."

## Even if You Achieve the American Dream, That Doesn't Necessarily Mean Other Americans Will Accept You

A few years ago, I was working on my laptop in a hotel lobby, waiting for reception to process my booking. I wore leather boots, jeans, and a peacoat. A guest of the hotel approached me and began shouting in slow English (as if I couldn't understand otherwise) that he needed me to clean his room. I was 25, had an Ivy League degree, and had completed one of the most competitive programs for college graduates in the country. And yet still I was being confused for the maid.

I realized then that no matter how hard I played by the rules, some people would never see me as a person of academic and professional success. This, perhaps, is the most psychologically disheartening part of the American dream: Achieving it doesn't necessarily mean we can "transcend" racial stereotypes about who we are.

It just takes one look at the rhetoric by current politicians to know that as first-generation Americans, we are still not seen as "American" as others. As so many cases have illustrated recently, no matter how much we focus on proving them wrong, negative perceptions from others will continue to challenge our sense of self-worth.

For black immigrants or children of immigrants, this exclusionary messaging is even more obvious. Kari Mugo, a writer who immigrated to the US from Kenya when she was 18, expressed to me the disappointment she has felt trying to feel welcomed here: "It's really hard to make an argument for a place that doesn't want you, and shows that every single day. It's been 12 years since I came here, and each year I'm growing more and more disillusioned."

I still cherish my college years, and still feel immensely proud to call myself an Ivy League graduate. I am humbled by my parents' sacrifices that allowed me to live the comparatively privileged life I've had. I acknowledge that it is in part *because* of this privilege that I can offer a critique of the United States in the first place. My parents and other immigrant families who focused only on survival didn't have the luxury of being critical.

Yet having that luxury, I think it's important to vocalize that in the United States, living the dream is far more nuanced than we often make others believe. As Mugo told me, "My friends back in Kenya always receive the message that America is so great. But I always wonder why we don't ever tell the people back home what it's really like. We always give off the illusion that everything is fine, without also acknowledging the many ways life here is really, really hard."

I deeply respect the choices my parents made, and I'm deeply grateful for the opportunities the United States provided. But at this point in my family's journey, I am curious to see what happens when we begin exploring a different dream.

## Print Citations

**CMS:** Machado, Amanda. "My Immigrant Family Achieved the American Dream: Then I Started to Question It." In *The Reference Shelf: The American Dream*, edited by Annette Calzone, 65-70. Ipswich, MA: H.W. Wilson, 2018.

**MLA:** Machado, Amanda. "My Immigrant Family Achieved the American Dream: Then I Started to Question It." *The Reference Shelf: The American Dream*. Ed. Annette Calzone. Ipswich: H.W. Wilson, 2018. 65-70. Print.

**APA:** Machado, A. (2018). My immigrant family achieved the American Dream: Then I started to question it. In Annette Calzone (Ed.), *The reference shelf: The American Dream* (pp. 65-70). Ipswich, MA: H.W. Wilson. (Original work published 2017)

# The Racial Wealth Gap and Today's American Dream

By Erin Currier and Sheida Elmi

*The Pew Charitable Trusts*, February 16, 2018

There is a growing recognition among Americans that moving up the income ladder in the United States can be challenging: As recently as 2014, only 23 percent of Americans believed that it's common for someone to start poor, work hard, and become rich, which was down 16 percentage points from just five years earlier.

The data back up this perception, making clear that many Americans born into the bottom fifth of the economic ladder never make it to the middle, let alone the top. The problem is particularly acute for families of color—and especially African American families—who are not always able to climb the economic ladder in the same way as their white peers. In 2014, 51 percent of respondents to the nationally representative Survey of American Family Finances, conducted by The Pew Charitable Trusts, said their households were financially secure. But there were significant differences by race: While 54 percent of white households reported feeling financially secure, the figure dropped to 37 percent for black households.

Perhaps not surprisingly, then, one key metric of financial security—liquid savings, or money held in checking and savings accounts, unused balances on prepaid cards, and cash saved at home—also differs drastically by race. While the typical white household, in Pew research from 2014, had 31 days of income in such savings, the typical black household had just five days' worth.

The racial gap goes beyond liquid savings, extending to financial assets—investments and retirement savings in addition to liquid savings—as well. In 2014, a quarter of black households would have less than $5 if they liquidated such assets, compared with the bottom 25 percent of white households—which would have as much as $3,000 after asset liquidation. And though having at least one household member with a college degree improves all family balance sheets, the benefits of education are also unevenly distributed by race and family structure. Among survey respondents who were college-educated, in a couple, and had no children, typical white respondents in 2014 had more than three

> Many Americans born into the bottom fifth of the economic ladder never make it to the middle, let alone the top.

times the wealth—a household's total assets minus total debts—than their black counterparts. A similar gap holds for homeownership—a main driver of wealth—in the United States: According to the U.S. Census Bureau, the white homeownership rate as of the fourth quarter of 2017 was 72.7 percent, while the black homeownership rate was 42.1 percent—the largest such disparity since World War II.

These household differences roll up to the community level, where families often live next to people of the same race and with similar education and income levels—creating neighborhoods segregated by socio-economic status. In fact, Pew research has shown that three-quarters of the residents of low-poverty neighborhoods are white, compared with just a third of those in high-poverty communities. Likewise, researchers at UCLA have found that schools in the South are now as segregated as they were about 50 years ago. This matters because research by Pew and others has shown that metro areas with the highest rates of economic segregation also experience the lowest rates of economic mobility; their residents are less likely to move up and down the income ladder over time than are those in areas with more economic integration.

The Generation X population in the United States, born between 1965 and 1980, provides more evidence of a racial gap in economic mobility, which is influenced by many factors, including family structure and educational attainment as well as race. Gen Xers are now adults in their prime working years, so they're likely to have completed their education and started families—and research shows that theirs may be the first generation in recent U.S. history to fall behind previous generations in wealth accumulation. Race is critical in this story: Simply put, Gen Xers raised at the top of the income ladder—by financially comfortable, well-educated parents, almost all of whom are white—become financially comfortable and well-educated themselves; Gen Xers raised at the bottom of the ladder have the opposite family background and economic outcome, and are statistically far more likely to be black than those at the top of the ladder. Four in 10 Gen Xers who remain at the bottom of the economic ladder, in fact, are black.

The persistent wealth gap between black and white households remains a challenge, especially as the U.S. population becomes more racially diverse. The data serve as a call to action for policymakers, community leaders, employers, and philanthropists to work together to find ways to create a more equitable system for this ever more diverse population. There will be no single, simple solution. The answers will be complex and difficult. But the time has come to identify the programs and policies that can help families improve their financial lives—and promote economic mobility for all.

## Print Citations

**CMS:** Currier, Erin, and Sheida Elmi. "The Racial Wealth Gap and Today's American Dream." In *The Reference Shelf: The American Dream*, edited by Annette Calzone, 71-73. Ipswich, MA: H.W. Wilson, 2018.

**MLA:** Currier, Erin, and Sheida Elmi. "The Racial Wealth Gap and Today's American Dream." *The Reference Shelf: The American Dream*. Ed. Annette Calzone. Ipswich: H.W. Wilson, 2018. 71-73. Print.

**APA:** Currier, E., & Elmi, S. (2018). The racial wealth gap and today's American dream. In Annette Calzone (Ed.), *The reference shelf: The American Dream* (pp. 71-73). Ipswich, MA: H.W. Wilson. (Original work published 2018)

# Why Blacks Believe in the American Dream More Than Whites

By Tami Luhby
*CNN Money*, November 25, 2015

Their family wealth is typically one-tenth that of whites. They earn considerably less. They are more likely to be unemployed or in poverty and they are less likely to own a home.

Yet despite all this, blacks and Hispanics are far more optimistic about being able to live the American Dream these days than whites.

Some 55% of blacks and 52% of Hispanics say it's easier for them to achieve the American Dream than it was for their parents, compared to 35% of whites, according to a new CNN/Kaiser Family Foundation poll on race.

This is true even though many blacks and Hispanics CNNMoney interviewed said they are not in a financial position to fulfill their own dreams anytime soon—if ever. For them, however, it's about opportunity. And they feel they have a lot more of it than their parents did.

Take Breionne Carter, a 22-year-old black woman who lives in Pflugerville, Texas, a suburb of Austin.

After working at Popeye's for three years, she just landed a full-time job with benefits at Dairy Queen and hopes to be promoted to manager in coming months. She plans to enter Austin Community College once she is more financially settled and can buy a car.

Carter doesn't know exactly what she wants to do in life, but her dream is to create companies that focus on things she likes—including clothes and music—that will also provide those in her community with jobs and other opportunities. She wants to encourage people to have more confidence and pride in themselves. "You have to keep going forward, no matter what's holding you back," she said.

Though she is strapped for cash now, Carter has no doubt she'll be able to achieve any goal she sets. A high school graduate with no children, she's thankful to be in a far different situation than her mother, whom she said faced more struggles as a darker skinned black woman who had her first of nine children at the age of 17 and dropped out of high school. (She eventually got her GED and now works in medical billing.)

Her mother told her stories of being spit on at work and being called the "N-word." Carter said she's doesn't feel judged on the color of her skin.

"The world is changing," said Carter. "I face less discrimination. I have the opportunity to do things she couldn't do."

It's not surprising that blacks and Hispanics say

**Some 55% of blacks and 52% of Hispanics say it's easier for them to achieve the American Dream than it was for their parents, compared to 35% of whites.**

they have a better chance of getting ahead today than their parents, experts said.

Previous generations of blacks had to contend with segregation and closed doors in many parts of the country. "[They] were bound by a set of legal and institutional restrictions," said Margaret Simms, director of the Low-Income Working Families project at the Urban Institute. There are "more possibilities for mobility than a generation or two ago."

Many Hispanics, meanwhile, migrated to this country or are the children or grandchildren of immigrants. They often see their fortunes rise with every generation, said Carol Graham, a Brookings Institution senior fellow whose research has also found blacks and Hispanics to be more optimistic about the future than whites.

But faith in the American Dream has withered in recent years. The Great Recession and weak economic recovery has left many families struggling. A 2009 Pew Charitable Trusts poll found that 63% of blacks and 62% of Hispanics said it was easier for them to achieve the dream than their parents, compared to 46% of whites.

Ray Sanchez, however, remains a firm believer in the dream, even though his personal finances have suffered in the last few years.

Sanchez, who is Hispanic, made good money touring the country as a Buddy Holly impersonator until 2011, when he aged out of the role. Now 51, he's unemployed and finding it hard to land a job because of his severe diabetes, which has left him with neuropathy. His family—which includes a son in 5th grade and a daughter in 11th grade, both on the honor roll—depends on his wife's income as a health care aide. He also has a 28-year-old daughter who lives several hours away from his Monmouth, Oregon, home.

For Sanchez, the American Dream is about having a happy and loving family and a president he trusts. Right now, he says he's content on both fronts...though the 2016 election may alter that.

His life stands in sharp contrast to his parents' experience. His father, who was of Mexican descent, was forced to live on the streets in Texas at the age of 7, after his mother (Sanchez's grandmother) abandoned the family and his father died. Sanchez's father had to teach himself to read and write. Eventually, he found work at a lumber mill. Sanchez's mother dropped out of high school and became an "average housewife," raising three children, he said.

So while times are tough at the moment, Sanchez is hopeful he can change his fortunes.

"I have an education, so I have a lot of options," Sanchez said, while watching his son play soccer. "I could go back to school. If one thing doesn't work, I can do something else."

Whites, however, aren't as optimistic about their chances of living the American Dream. That's likely because many of their parents were able to buy homes and send their kids to college, possibly even on one income.

"They are starting from a place where they were much more comfortable," Simms said.

Jon Burke's parents were able to achieve their American Dream and were more confident they could hold onto it. But Burke, a 34 year old white man, can't say the same about his own situation.

While he's financially stable, he is less certain about the future. A legal aid lawyer in Harvard, Massachusetts, he is raising three children with his wife, a lawyer in a private practice. Child care is expensive. Health care is expensive. College, even at a state school, is expensive, he says. The family's finances could go downhill quickly if someone gets sick or loses their job.

Americans have far less certainty and face more challenges these days—partly because of the decline of unions and changes in government policies—than many did in his parents' generation, Burke said.

His father was a college professor and his mom was a high school teacher. They had job security, guaranteed pensions and free healthcare. Now, people must shoulder too much of the risk and the burdens, rather than being spread across society, he says. The American Dream is too focused on individual achievement, he said.

"You could be doing fine today, but down the road, not so much," said Burke. "There are a lot of unnecessary obstacles people have to overcome. I don't think my parents had them in the past."

## Print Citations

**CMS:** Luhby, Tami. "Why Blacks Believe in the American Dream More Than Whites." In *The Reference Shelf: The American Dream*, edited by Annette Calzone, 74-76. Ipswich, MA: H.W. Wilson, 2018.

**MLA:** Luhby, Tami. "Why Blacks Believe in the American Dream More Than Whites." *The Reference Shelf: The American Dream*. Ed. Annette Calzone. Ipswich: H.W. Wilson, 2018. 74-76. Print.

**APA:** Luhby, T. (2018). Why blacks believe in the American dream more than whites. In Annette Calzone (Ed.), *The reference shelf: The American Dream* (pp. 74-76). Ipswich, MA: H.W. Wilson. (Original work published 2015)

# A Federal College Loan Program Is Exacerbating the Racial Wealth Gap

By Dwyer Gunn
*Pacific Standard*, May 18, 2018

In America today, the average white family currently holds almost seven times the wealth of the average African-American family, and five times the wealth of the average Hispanic family. This disparity is nothing new: The racial wealth gap hasn't changed in 50 years, despite decades of policies aimed at reducing discrimination in the labor market and improving African Americans' access to higher education.

The causes behind this wealth gap, while not simple, are clear: Centuries of slavery, segregation, and government-sanctioned discrimination dramatically curtailed African-American families' ability to amass wealth and pass it along to their children. All the while, white families were slowly accumulating wealth, thanks in part to government policies designed to help them afford college tuition and a home mortgage, and to later pass such benefits on to their children. As William Darity, a professor at Duke University, told me last month, "[t]hese inequalities are baked into the system through the process of transfers that take place across generations."

A new report from Rachel Fishman of the New America Foundation, a nonpartisan Washington, D.C., think tank, highlights yet another federal government program that's similarly widening the wealth gap: the Parent PLUS loan program. The Parent PLUS program was created in 1980, its primary goal to help middle-income families pay for college during an era of high interest rates and increasing tuition. The loans, which are not subject to the borrowing limits on other types of college loans, carry a higher interest rate than student loans and are typically used by parents only after other kinds of financial aid and loans (i.e., student loans, federal subsidized and unsubsidized loans, etc.) are tapped out.

Indeed, the majority of Parent PLUS borrowers fit this profile. . . . From the report, over 50 percent of borrowers in 2012 had a family income over $75,000.

Among white borrowers, the Parent PLUS program appears to work as intended (i.e., as a financing mechanism for wealthier families). Among white families, the share of PLUS borrowers increases alongside income: Only one in 10 white PLUS borrowers in 2012 had a family income less than $30,000, and a third had an income over $110,000. Among black families, however, the opposite is true: a third of black PLUS borrowers in 2012 had an income under $30,000, while one-in-10 had an income over $110,000.

Fishman finds a similar disparity for families with an expected family contribution (EFC) of $0. The EFC, which is calculated when determining eligibility for various forms of financial aid, is meant to indicate how much money a family can contribute to their child's education. Families with an EFC of $0 are typically quite low-income and, by definition, cannot afford to contribute anything to their children's education. As Fishman writes, "[a]rguably, no family with a zero EFC should take on a PLUS loan, as EFC is a rough approximation of the ability to repay a loan."

> **America's retreat from public financing for higher education has disproportionately harmed African-American families.**

Nonetheless, . . . 33 percent of black PLUS borrowers in 2012 came from families with a $0 EFC, compared to only 9 percent of white PLUS borrowers.

Perhaps not surprisingly, all this borrowing adds up to significant disparities in total family indebtedness, particularly among the poorest families.

"Black families with zero EFC accumulated an average of $33,721 in intergenerational debt, of which $11,352 was in PLUS loans," Fishman concludes. "By contrast, white families with zero EFC accumulated $25,434 in debt, 25 percent less. Even among families that the EFC formula judges equally needy, debt outcomes for white and Black families are very different."

So how, in Fishman's words, did the Parent PLUS loan program go so far off the rails and "end up serving exactly who it was meant to for white families but not families of color, especially Black families?" Fishman points to all the usual known drivers of the racial wealth gap—discriminatory housing policies, labor market discrimination, etc.—that have put African-American families in the difficult situation of having few other options for funding their children's education, but she makes another point as well: America's retreat from public financing for higher education has disproportionately harmed African-American families.

As Sara Goldrick-Rab documented in exhaustive and devastating detail in her 2016 book, the federal financial aid system has simply failed to keep up with the demand for, and cost of, higher education. Pell grants, which were created to allow low-income Americans to go to college without wracking up tons of debt, no longer cover even community college tuition in many places, let alone living expenses or the tuition costs at more expensive institutions. Public institutions of higher education, meanwhile, have responded to education funding cuts by increasing tuition. These trends, while painful for middle-class white families as well, have been disastrous for black families with much less familial wealth to draw on. . .

Fishman's findings are all the more concerning in light of the ample body of evidence concluding that black students are much more likely to struggle to repay back their student loans. In a report for the Brookings Institution, the researcher Judith Scott-Clayton projected that 70 percent of black student borrowers may ultimately default on their loans and concluded that "[d]ebt and default among black college students is at crisis levels."

Fishman's report proposes a number of feasible, short-term reforms to the PLUS program—things like improving counseling, disclosure, and servicing procedures around the loans—but she ultimately concludes that a true fix must be much bigger.

"The federal government's role in higher education is important, and it already provides grants and loans to help students afford it, but that is not enough," Fishman writes. "In order to provide true access for low-wealth families, there must be a targeted investment that is not debt-financed and will completely bring down the cost of, at a minimum, public two- and four-year universities while holding institutions accountable for that investment."

## Print Citations

**CMS:** Gunn, Dwyer. "A Federal College Loan Program Is Exacerbating the Racial Wealth Gap." In *The Reference Shelf: The American Dream,* edited by Annette Calzone, 77-79. Ipswich, MA: H.W. Wilson, 2018.

**MLA:** Gunn, Dwyer. "A Federal College Loan Program Is Exacerbating the Racial Wealth Gap." *The Reference Shelf: The American Dream.* Ed. Annette Calzone. Ipswich: H.W. Wilson, 2018. 77-79. Print.

**APA:** Gunn, D. (2018). A federal college loan program is exacerbating the racial wealth gap. In Annette Calzone (Ed.), *The reference shelf: The American Dream* (pp. 77-79). Ipswich, MA: H.W. Wilson. (Original work published 2018)

# Where Slavery Thrived, Inequality Rules Today

By Stephanie Mihm

*The Boston Globe*, August 24, 2014

Earlier this month Standard and Poor's Rating Services, a credit rating firm that rarely weighs in on social issues, published a scathing report on income inequality and social mobility in the United States. The firm warned that current levels of inequality were "dampening" growth, and predicted that "inequalities will extend into the next generation, with diminished opportunities for upward social mobility."

This unusual report on inequality, like Thomas Piketty's best-selling book on the same subject, addresses unequal fortunes, declining mobility, and stagnating economic growth as national or even global problems, which demand similarly large-scale solutions. But scholars are also well aware that these problems vary greatly from place to place. Consider a recent, much-publicized study of social mobility by economist Raj Chetty and his colleagues at Harvard and Berkeley. As the illuminating map generated by that study shows, children born in some regions—Salt Lake City and San Jose, Calif., for example—have a reasonable shot of moving up the social ladder. By contrast, many parts of the former Confederacy, it seems, are now the places where the American dream goes to die.

Why is that true? At first blush, you might guess race could explain the variation. When the study's authors crunched the data, they found that the larger the black population in any given county, the lower the overall social mobility. But there was more to the story than blacks unable to break the cycle of poverty. In a passing comment, Chetty and his co-authors observed that "both blacks and whites living in areas with large African-American populations have lower rates of upward income mobility." Far from being divergent, the fates of poor blacks and poor whites in these regions are curiously, inextricably, intertwined.

Instead of chalking it up to race, recent research points toward a more startling and somewhat controversial explanation: When we see broad areas of inequality in America today, what we are actually seeing is the lingering stain of slavery. Since 2002, with increasing refinement in the years since, economic historians have argued that the "peculiar institution," as it was once called, is dead but not gone. Today, in the 21st century, it still casts an economic shadow over both blacks and whites: "Slavery," writes Harvard economist Nathan Nunn, "had a long-term effect on inequality as well as income."

His work is representative of a new, more historical direction within economics. Its proponents believe that institutions devised centuries ago tend to persist, structuring economic reality in the 21st century in ways that are largely invisible. Their hope is that, by tracing these connections between past and present, they may be able to point the way toward more effective solutions to today's seemingly intractable economic problems.

In 2002, two economic historians, Stanley Engerman and Kenneth Sokoloff, published an influential paper that tried to answer a vexing question: why are some countries in the Americas defined by far more extreme and enduring levels of inequality—and by extension, limited social mobility and economic underdevelopment—than others?

The answer, they argued, lay in the earliest history of each country's settlement. The political and social institutions put in place then tended to perpetuate the status quo. They concluded that societies that began "with extreme inequality tended to adopt institutions that served to advantage members of the elite and hamper social mobility." This, they asserted, resulted in economic underdevelopment over the long run.

More specifically, they observed that regions where sugar could be profitably grown invariably gave rise to societies defined by extreme inequality. The reason, they speculated, had to do with the fact that large-scale sugar plantations made intensive use of slave labor, generating institutions that privileged a small elite of white planters over a majority of black slaves. These institutions, their later work suggested, could encompass everything from property rights regimes to tax structures to public schools.

Harvard economist Nathan Nunn offered a more detailed statistical analysis of this "Engerman-Sokoloff hypothesis" in a paper first published in 2008. His research confirmed that early slave use in the Americas was correlated with poor long-term growth. More specifically, he examined county-level data on slavery and inequality in the United States, and found a robust correlation between past reliance on slave labor and both economic underdevelopment and contemporary inequality. He disagreed with Engerman and Sokoloff's claim that it was only large-scale plantation slavery that generated these effects; rather, he found, any kind of slavery seemed to have begotten long-term economic woes.

Nunn also offered a more precise explanation for present-day troubles. In Engerman and Sokoloff's narrative, slavery led to inequality, which led to economic underdevelopment. But when Nunn examined levels of inequality in 1860—as measured by holdings of land—these proved a poor predictor of future problems. Only the presence of slavery was a harbinger of problems. "It is not economic inequality that caused the subsequent development of poor institutions," wrote Nunn. "Rather, it was slavery itself."

This finding was echoed in a study by Brazilian economists Rodrigo Soares, Juliano Assunção, and Tomás Goulart published in the *Journal of Comparative Economics* in 2012. Soares and his colleagues examined the connection between historical slavery and contemporary inequality in a number of countries, largely in Latin

America. The authors found a consistent correlation between the existence—and intensity—of slavery in the past and contemporary inequality. Moreover, this relationship was independent of the number of people of African descent living there today. As Soares said in an interview, "Societies that used more slavery are not more unequal simply because they have relatively more black people."

The question, then, is how exactly did slavery have this effect on contemporary inequality? Soares and his colleagues speculated that limited political rights for slaves and their descendants played a role, as did negligible access to credit and capital. Racial discrimination, too, would have played a part, though this would not explain why whites born in former slaveholding regions might find themselves subject to higher levels of inequality. Nunn, though, advanced an additional explanation, pointing to an idea advanced by Stanford economic historian Gavin Wright in 2006.

In lands turned over to slavery, Wright had observed, there was little incentive to provide so-called public goods—schools, libraries, and other institutions—that attract migrants. In the North, by contrast, the need to attract and retain free labor in areas resulted in a far greater investment in public goods—institutions that would, over the succeeding decades, offer far greater opportunities for social mobility and lay the foundation for sustained, superior economic growth.

> **The fates of poor blacks and poor whites in these regions are curiously, inextricably, intertwined.**

As it happens, a contemporary critic of slavery took it upon himself to measure some of these differences between North and South. In 1857, a Southerner named Hinton Rowan Helper published an incendiary book titled *The Impending Crisis.* Though a virulent racist, Helper was no friend of slavery, and he quantified in excruciating detail the relative number of schools, libraries, and other institutions in both free and slaveholding states, finding time and again that his region failed to measure up to the North.

In Pennsylvania he found 393 public libraries, but in South Carolina, a mere 26. In the South, he observed, "the common school-house, the poor man's college, is hardly known, showing how little interest is felt in the chief treasures of the State, the immortal minds of the multitude who are not born to wealth."

***

What someone like Helper may not have foreseen is that the abolition of slavery would not cure these ills. The destruction of slavery did not destroy all the political institutions, social mores, and cultural traditions that sustained it. Nor did it make public institutions, of the kind that the north had been building for decades, suddenly come into being.

This notion about the "persistence" of economic institutions is part of a larger dialogue within economics. Economists ranging from MIT's Daron Acemoglu to Harvard's Melissa Fisher have examined how institutions and practices adopted centuries ago can shape economic reality. But not everyone buys the idea that the past can structure the present in such an enduring, predictable fashion. Wright is among the critics of this approach; he is skeptical of Engerman and Sokoloff's hypothesis. "The persistence of inequality per se is a myth," he says, pointing to research that highlights the degree to which inequality has ebbed and flowed in Latin America.

Wright counts himself "unconvinced" regarding comparable claims about the United States. "No doubt slavery has played some kind of background role," he concedes. But he sees the relationship between historical slavery and contemporary inequality as an interesting correlation, not a directly causal one. Correlating one variable with another across the centuries "isn't the same as writing history," he notes. "If you don't connect the dots, you're just groping."

Another criticism of the "persistence" school is that it may justify passivity. If counties or countries have always been poor or unequal because of something that happened so long ago, what chance do contemporary policy makers have at deflecting the dead hand of the past?

But there is room for hope, as Wright's own research would suggest. In *Sharing the Prize*, an economic history of the civil rights movement published in 2013, Wright found that efforts to end discrimination paid substantial, enduring benefits to black Southerners. Perhaps more surprisingly, he found that the movement benefited whites, too. Many poorer whites found that that the destruction of the old order—the end of poll taxes, for example—ushered in increased levels of public funding for schools, newfound political power, and a host of other economic, political, and educational benefits, particularly in the years immediately following the passage of the Civil Rights Act.

That revolution, of course, is still a work in progress. As we've been reminded over the last two weeks by the clashes in Ferguson, Mo., between mostly black protesters and a mostly white police force, there's a long way to go before the vestiges of slavery are fully and finally made a thing of the past. But this new body of research may help us grasp that solutions to persistent inequality will require more focused policies. Increasing the level of food stamps, as economist Paul Krugman has suggested, might help, but it is perhaps too diffuse and indiscriminate a solution.

Instead, the best way to deal with the lingering effects of dead institutions like slavery may be to create regional institutions aimed to promoting social mobility and economic growth. Georgia, for example, has tried to level the field with the "HOPE Scholarship," which enables high schoolers with a "B" average or higher to attend in-state public colleges and universities for free and private in-state schools at a heavy discount.

Such programs, with some modifications, could go a long way toward promoting social mobility in the former slaveholding regions of the United States. That's not to say that the problems will be easy to solve. But the progress we've already made, both politically and economically, would suggest that while we may live in slavery's shadow, we are not prisoners of the past, either.

## Print Citations

**CMS:** Mihm, Stephanie. "Where Slavery Thrived, Inequality Rules Today." In *The Reference Shelf: The American Dream*, edited by Annette Calzone, 80-84. Ipswich, MA: H.W. Wilson, 2018.

**MLA:** Mihm, Stephanie. "Where Slavery Thrived, Inequality Rules Today." *The Reference Shelf: The American Dream*. Ed. Annette Calzone. Ipswich: H.W. Wilson, 2018. 80-84. Print.

**APA:** Mihm, S. (2018). Where slavery thrived, inequality rules today. In Annette Calzone (Ed.), *The reference shelf: The American Dream* (pp. 80-84). Ipswich, MA: H.W. Wilson. (Original work published 2014)

# 4

# The American Dream Over Time

By Andrew Lichtenstein/Corbis via Getty Images

Homeless person on Manhattan's midtown Avenue of the Americas, January 2016. In the 2010s, more and more Americans have become skeptical of the American Dream, following the 2008 Great Recession and the mortgage crisis. They have begun reflecting on the meaning of the dream, which historically encompassed more than building wealth and included the idea of an egalitarian society for all, one in which individuals can reach their highest potential.

# Transforming the Dream

For many of the millions of immigrants who came to the United States from the mid-1800s to the early 1900s, the American dream was about accruing sufficient wealth to take care of their families and improve their positions back in their native nations. But there has always been another element to the American dream as well, the dream of finding freedom, security, and happiness in a new home. The unusual history of the American dream exists at the intersection of both of these ideas, America as a home and America as an opportunity.

## A National Dream

The term "American dream" appears in several different forms in writings from the early 1900s, but the phrase didn't become popular until it was used in the 1931 book *The American Epic* by financier-turned-historian James Truslow Adams. In his book, Adams defines the American dream as: "a dream of a social order in which each man and each woman shall be able to attain to the fullest stature of which they are innately capable, and be recognized by others for what they are, regardless of the fortuitous circumstances of birth or position."[1]

In the 2010s, as more and more Americans have become skeptical of the American dream, Adams's unbridled optimism might seem outdated. In many ways, it can be argued that America failed to embody the principles and philosophy that Adams envisioned in the years since he popularized the idea of a national "dream" of a better life. However, Adams's personal history helps to explain why he was uniquely positioned to see the promise of America's cultural environment.

Adams was born in Brooklyn and was intimately familiar with the immigrant's journey, as his paternal grandmother was Spanish and his father was from Venezuela. However, Adams didn't live the life familiar to many of the nation's struggling immigrants then or now. Born into a wealthy family, Adams enjoyed a comfortable childhood and had the resources needed to invest in his future, thanks to his family's success. Adams entered finance and, though he was wholly dispassionate about the field, he earned an income sufficient enough that in 1921, after 12 years as a businessman, he retired to pursue his passion: history.

Adams's books sold well because of his different approach. Instead of writing history for academic audiences, he leaned into his status as an academic outsider, writing history in a language more tuned to the popular press. He talked about how ordinary Americans lived their lives through history, and this enabled him to connect with the public in a way that few historians had been able to achieve.[2] Unlike the many historians who had covered the history of New England, Adams concentrated on unusual stories of individuals, groups, and cities rarely covered by academics interested in the region or era. It was the beginning of an academic approach now called "social history," which became a popular subset of historical writing into the twenty-first century.

In his coverage of early New England history, Adams was at his most unique. While the standard historical version of events always cast the Puritans as religious activists seeking the freedom to practice their faith away from the oppressive clutches of the Church of England, Adams focused on the more practical reasons for the Puritan's journey. He was the first historian to describe the Puritans as immigrants not dissimilar from those arriving in the nation in the 1930s, suggesting that the Puritans came to America seeking economic opportunities as much as anything else. Adams thereby celebrated the immigrant story, seeing it as part and parcel of America itself, and so paved the way for scholars like Bernard Baylyn and John F. Kennedy, who would write influential histories in later years aimed also at highlighting the history of American colonization as a history of immigration.[3]

Adams's *The American Epic* became a bestseller after it was published in 1931, even though, America was in the grips of the most severe economic crisis that the nation had ever seen. From the stock market crash on October 27, 1929, the Depression worsened each year. There were no social nets in place to keep people from sliding into abject poverty. Even families on a seemingly solid upward trajectory in the years before the Depression were vulnerable to complete economic collapse. The suicide rate increased from 12 to 18.9 per 100,000 as many sank into psychological depression, unable to find work and uncertain how to care for their families.[4] That Adams's *American Epic* came out during the Great Depression is ironic, and even his publisher had doubts about the book's success given what was happening in the nation. But it may have been the Depression itself that shaped Adams' vision.

In *The American Epic*, Adams is careful to differentiate between his definition of the American dream and what he characterized as the shallow race for wealth in which many Americans were engaged. In his view, the American dream was not about fancy cars or living a life of luxury, but rather about creating a society in which people were able to find their way to their ideal place. This reflected Adams's successful transition from businessman to historian, but also his reflection of the immigrant experience. In many ways, Adams was a critic of what he saw as an increasingly materialistic American culture that ignored the true promise of America. Rather than a place simply to earn one's fortune, Adams envisioned America as a social experiment for a more egalitarian society and, in a moment when many Americans were losing hope in their dream of economic realization, his vision of innate realization resounded with many Americans.

## Having a Dream

A national "dream" is a unique thing for a country to have. No other nation has adopted one, though many have adopted something similar to a national ethos. The fact that America not only has what its citizens perceive as characteristic values and principles but that these values and principles constitute a singularly individual dream of American society is, in many ways, a function of the way that immigration shaped America. Because America is a nation populated primarily by immigrants, the goals and hopes of immigrants, seeking change, improvement, new opportunities, and, in general, a better life, became ensconced in the American imagination as representative of the country itself.

In many ways, the American dream is an example of American exceptionalism, the idea that America is wholly unique and, in many ways, more advanced than the other nations, especially concerning concepts like freedom and democracy. Some express exceptionalism through their belief that America has a global mission, usually defined as spreading democracy or freedom. Others express exceptionalism through the belief that any feature of the world, from language to art to politics to society itself, has reached or at least will reach its most complete, most advanced expression only in America.

Exceptionalism also means, for many Americans, devotion to a host of characteristics that they see as necessarily part of what makes America great. For instance, some might believe that America is great because Americans work harder. A Gallup Poll from 2014 found that Americans work longer hours than in many other parts of the world, with full-time workers working an average of 47 hours per week, while average workweeks in Germany and Sweden are closer to 35 hours. Other studies have shown that American workers rarely take vacation days, even when available, rarely take family leave, and rarely take time off from work during the work day.[5] The way that many Americans interpret the American dream is that hard work equals success and that the harder one works, the better off one will be. Many Americans take pride in being self-styled "workaholics" and criticize other countries for being "lazy." The question is, what has the American work ethic done for American well-being?

While many Americans see the American dream as being about prosperity, and the ability to achieve a better life for oneself and one's family, many Americans are today far less optimistic that America provides these opportunities. A Pew Research report from 2014 found that only 30 percent of Americans were optimistic about their future, and about their ability to achieve the "dream." By contrast, in Vietnam, a country that has a fraction of the wealth and in which a much higher percentage of the population lives nearer to poverty, 94 percent were optimistic about the future. Furthermore, while 75 percent of Americans listed "hard work" as the key to getting ahead, in many other nation's respondents listed family and community as the most important determinants.[6] In terms of poverty rates, economic mobility, and income equality, America now lags behind many of the economically advanced nations of the world, including all of Western Europe, and increasingly resembles a developing nation in terms of broader income inequality.

In the twenty-first century, every American has his or her own version of the American dream, but nearly all versions contain some sense that America is a place in which to pursue a better life. This core essence of the American dream is similar to what Adams imagined, and yet the nuance of Adams' message, of a collectivism and a social order, has largely been lost over time. Ironically, though Adams popularized the concept of the American dream, the mainstream concept of the dream that persists today more closely resembles that which Adams criticized, a contest for self-realization rather than a platform for the betterment of society.

## Works Used

Abadi, Mark. "6 American Work Habits People in Other Countries Think Are Ridiculous." *Independent*. Independent Media. Nov 17, 2017. Retrieved from https://www.independent.co.uk/news/business/american-work-habits-us-countries-job-styles-hours-hoilday-a8060616.html.

DiBacco, Thomas V. "How a History Professor Became a Newspaper Columnist." *Orlando Sentinel*. Tronc, Inc.. Jun 22, 2018. Retrieved from http://www.orlandosentinel.com/opinion/os-ed-history-professor-to-newspaper-columnist-20180612-story.html.

Egan, Matt. "America More Pessimistic Than Poor Nations." *CNN*. CNN Money. Oct 9, 2014. Retrieved from https://money.cnn.com/2014/10/09/news/economy/poor-nations-more-optimistic-than-united-states/index.html.

"James Truslow Adams Papers, 1918-1949." *Columbia University Libraries*. Archival Collections. 2018. Retrieved from http://www.columbia.edu/cu/lweb/archival/collections/ldpd_4078384/.

McElvaine, Robert S. *The Great Depression: American, 1929-1941*." New York: Times Books, 1993.

Widmer, Ted. "What the Man Behind the 'American Dream' Really Meant." *Boston Globe*. Boston Globe Media Partners, LLC. Apr 16, 2015. Retrieved from https://www.bostonglobe.com/ideas/2015/04/16/what-man-behind-american-dream-really-meant/uni438RcM82Y3QDnkwRz5H/story.html.

Wills, Matthew, "James Truslow Adams: Dreaming Up the American Dream." *Jstory Daily*. JSTOR. May 18, 2015. Retrieved from https://daily.jstor.org/james-truslow-adams-dreaming-american-dream/.

## Notes

1. Wills, "James Truslow Adams: Dreaming Up the American Dream."
2. DiBacco, "How a History Professor Became a Newspaper Columnist."
3. Widmer, "What the Man Behind the 'American Dream' Really Meant."
4. McElvaine, *The Great Depression: America, 1929-1941*.
5. Abadi, "6 American Work Habits People in Other Countries Think Are Ridiculous."
6. Egan, "America More Pessimistic Than Poor Nations."

# The Transformation of the "American Dream"

By Robert J. Shiller

*The New York Times*, August 4, 2017

"The American Dream is back." President Trump made that claim in a speech in January.

They are ringing words, but what do they mean? Language is important, but it can be slippery. Consider that the phrase, the American Dream, has changed radically through the years.

Mr. Trump and Ben Carson, the secretary of housing and urban development, have suggested it involves owning a beautiful home and a roaring business, but it wasn't always so. Instead, in the 1930s, it meant freedom, mutual respect and equality of opportunity. It had more to do with morality than material success.

This drift in meaning is significant, because the American Dream—and international variants like the Australian Dream, Le Rêve Français and others — represents core values. In the United States, these values affect major government decisions on housing, regulation and mortgage guarantees, and millions of private choices regarding whether to start a business, buy an ostentatious home or rent an apartment.

Conflating the American dream with expensive housing has had dangerous consequences: It may have even contributed to the last housing bubble, the one that led to the financial crisis of 2008-9.

These days, Mr. Trump is using the hallowed phrase in pointed ways. In his January speech, he framed the slogan as though it were an entrepreneurial aspiration. "We are going to create an environment for small business like we haven't seen in many many decades," he said, adding, "So, essentially, we are getting rid of regulations to a massive extent, could be as much as 75 percent."

Mr. Carson has explicitly said that homeownership is a central part of the Dream. In a speech at the National Housing Conference on June 9, he said, "I worry that millennials may become a lost generation for homeownership, excluded from the American Dream."

But that wasn't what the American Dream entailed when the writer James Truslow Adams popularized it in 1931, in his book *The Epic of America*.

Mr. Adams emphasized ideals rather than material goods, a "dream of a land in which life should be better and richer and fuller for every man, with opportunity for each according to his ability or achievement." And he clarified, "It is not a dream of motor cars and high wages merely, but a dream of a social order in which each man and each woman shall be able to attain to the fullest stature of which they are innately capable, and recognized by others for what they are."

His achievement was an innovation in language that largely replaced the older terms "American character" and "American principles" with a forward-looking phrase that implied modesty about current success in giving respect and equal opportunity to all people. The American dream was a *trajectory* to a promising future, a model for the United States and for the whole world.

In the 1930s and '40s, the term appeared occasionally in advertisements for intellectual products: plays, books and church sermons, book reviews and high-minded articles. During these years, it rarely, if ever, referred to business success or homeownership.

By 1950, shortly after World War II and the triumph against fascism, it was still about freedom and equality. In a book published in 1954, Peter Marshall, former chaplain of the United States Senate, defined the American Dream with spiritually resounding words: "Religious liberty to worship God according to the dictates of one's own conscience and equal opportunity for all men," he said, "are the twin pillars of the American Dream."

The term began to be used extensively in the 1960s. It may have owed its growing power to Martin Luther King's "I Have a Dream" speech in 1963, in which he spoke of a vision that was "deeply rooted in the American Dream." He said he dreamed of the disappearance of prejudice and a rise in community spirit, and certainly made no mention of deregulation or mortgage subsidies.

But as the term became more commonplace, its connection with notions of equality and community weakened. In the 1970s and '80s, home builders used it extensively in advertisements, perhaps to make conspicuous consumption seem patriotic.

Thanks in part to the deluge of advertisements, many people came to associate the American Dream with homeownership, with some unfortunate results. Increasing home sales became public policy. In 2003, President George W. Bush signed the American Dream Downpayment Act, subsidizing home purchases during a period in which a housing bubble — the one that would lead to the 2008-9

**Conflating the American dream with expensive housing has had dangerous consequences.**

financial crisis — was already growing at a 10 percent annual rate, according to the S.&P. Corelogic Case-Shiller U.S. National Home Price index (which I helped to create).

This year, *Forbes* magazine started what it calls the "American Dream Index." It is based on seven statistical measures of material prosperity: bankruptcies, building permits, entrepreneurship, goods-producing employment, labor participation rate, layoffs and unemployment claims. This kind of characterization is commonplace today, and very different from the original spirit of the American dream.

One thing is clear: Bringing back the fevered housing dream of a decade ago would not be in the public interest. In *House Lust: America's Obsession With Our Homes*, published in 2008, Daniel McGinn marveled at the craving for housing in that era: "In many neighborhoods, if you'd judged the nation's interests by its backyard-barbecue conversation — settings where subjects like war, death, and politics are risky conversational gambits — a lot of people find homes to be more compelling than any geopolitical struggle."

This is not to say that homes have no appropriate place in our dreams or our consciousness. To the contrary, in a 2015 book *Home: How Habitat Made Us Human*, the neuroanthropologist John S. Allen wrote, "We humans are a species of *homebodies*." Ever since humans began making stone tools and pottery, they have needed a place to store them, he says, and the potential for intense feelings about our homes has evolved.

But the last decade has shown that with a little encouragement, many can easily become excessively lustful about homeownership and wealth, to the detriment of our economy and society.

That's the wrong way to go. Instead, we need to bring back the American Dream of a just society, where everyone has an opportunity to reach "the fullest stature of which they are innately capable."

## Print Citations

**CMS:** Shiller, Robert J. "The Transformation of the 'American Dream.'" In *The Reference Shelf: The American Dream*, edited by Annette Calzone, 91-93. Ipswich, MA: H.W. Wilson, 2018.

**MLA:** Shiller, Robert J. "The Transformation of the 'American Dream.'" *The Reference Shelf: The American Dream*. Ed. Annette Calzone. Ipswich: H.W. Wilson, 2018. 91-93. Print.

**APA:** Shiller, R.J. (2018). The transformation of the "American Dream." In Annette Calzone (Ed.), *The reference shelf: The American Dream* (pp. 91-93). Ipswich, MA: H.W. Wilson. (Original work published 2017)

# The Economy Is Changing and So Is the American Dream

By Jared Meyer
*Forbes*, March 22, 2017

Since the rise of the internet, the world has witnessed more impressive levels of technological innovation than was ever thought possible. While this progress was quick to transform the American economy, government policy has struggled to keep pace.

Those entering the new economy are different as well. Many millennials have the desire to start their own businesses. Young voters' respect for entrepreneurship goes far beyond near-universal reverence for the late Steve Jobs. Polls consistently find that two-thirds of millennials want to work for themselves.

While the American dream may have once been finding employment at a large company, working there for a few decades and then retiring with a defined-benefit pension, millennials' American dream looks much different than that of their parents' and grandparents'. Young people prioritize new opportunities to change or advance their careers. And they prefer work that is individualized and flexible, which has become the model of the future for many occupations.

This model of being able to work wherever and whenever someone wants extends far beyond popular new economy services such as Uber and Lyft. Because of the newfound ability to reach customers through internet platforms, everyone from graphic designers to plumbers can connect with customers and market their businesses more cheaply and easily than ever before. This is one reason why millennials of all political leanings overwhelmingly support the sharing economy.

By providing a platform to connect people who want a service or product with people who are offering that service or product, the sharing economy has enabled transactions that would previously have been impossible. Sure, the internet made these specific business models possible—but the desire to make products more accessible, affordable, and convenient has existed for as long as trade itself.

People have always had the desire to buy a hard-to-find product, find a place to stay, eat a home-cooked meal, get assistance on a task, or find a way to get around. But it was often too time-consuming to find someone willing to offer the desired goods or services, especially at a reasonable price. For example, it would be completely impractical to go from door to door asking home owners if they have an extra room to rent and for how much. Now travelers simply log on to Airbnb and, with a few clicks of a mouse, they can find rooms that fit their needs and budgets.

> **Young people prioritize new opportunities to change or advance their careers. And they prefer work that is individualized and flexible.**

In the face of these benefits and high levels of public support, policymakers often fail to realize that this 21st century economy cannot flourish under a 20th century regulatory structure . Business owners and consumers alike are frustrated with bureaucrats' attempts to apply decades-old laws to regulate emerging technologies and industries that could not have been imagined when these laws were written.

For example, consider consumer protection regulation. A common justification for this type of regulation is the lack of information about a product or service that consumer can access. In today's age of Yelp, Amazon, Google Reviews, and Angie's List, it is difficult to argue that consumers suffer from a lack of information. Because of this increased access to information, even if businesses are unwilling to police themselves, customers can vet businesses and hold them accountable. Blogs, social media, and customer reviews all allow people to instantly find information about the products or services that they use and easily share their thoughts with others.

This fundamental shift in the economy is changing attitudes towards regulation. Only 18 percent of millennials believe regulators have the public's interest primarily in mind. Young people, influenced by the sharing economy's success and the subsequent hostile response of some policymakers, realize that many regulations protect special interests instead of public safety. They want companies to be held liable for harming consumers, but they do not support regulations that keep out new competition or dictate how entrepreneurs must meet their customers' needs.

Though regulatory fights over Uber and Airbnb constantly make the news, it is important to realize that the same trends that enabled these companies' business models will transform more than vehicle transportation and short-term lodging. Technology is going to continue making the workforce and marketplace more flexible, individualized, and mobile. Americans—especially millennials—are entrepreneurial by nature and innovations that make it easier for people to work for themselves while providing more options to consumers should be welcomed by policymakers.

## Print Citations

**CMS:** Meyer, Jared. "The Economy Is Changing and So Is the American Dream." In *The Reference Shelf: The American Dream*, edited by Annette Calzone, 94-96. Ipswich, MA: H.W. Wilson, 2018.

**MLA:** Meyer, Jared. "The Economy Is Changing and So Is the American Dream." *The Reference Shelf: The American Dream*. Ed. Annette Calzone. Ipswich: H.W. Wilson, 2018. 94-96. Print.

**APA:** Meyer, J. (2018). The economy is changing and so is the American dream. In Annette Calzone (Ed.), *The reference shelf: The American Dream* (pp. 94-96). Ipswich, MA: H.W. Wilson. (Original work published 2017)

# Rethinking the American Dream

By David Kamp
*Vanity Fair*, April, 2009

The year was 1930, a down one like this one. But for Moss Hart, it was the time for his particularly American moment of triumph. He had grown up poor in the outer boroughs of New York City—"the grim smell of actual want always at the end of my nose," he said—and he'd vowed that if he ever made it big he would never again ride the rattling trains of the city's dingy subway system. Now he was 25, and his first play, *Once in a Lifetime,* had just opened to raves on Broadway. And so, with three newspapers under his arm and a wee-hours celebration of a successful opening night behind him, he hailed a cab and took a long, leisurely sunrise ride back to the apartment in Brooklyn where he still lived with his parents and brother.

Crossing the Brooklyn Bridge into one of the several drab tenement neighborhoods that preceded his own, Hart later recalled, "I stared through the taxi window at a pinch-faced 10-year-old hurrying down the steps on some morning errand before school, and I thought of myself hurrying down the street on so many gray mornings out of a doorway and a house much the same as this one.... It was possible in this wonderful city for that nameless little boy—for any of its millions—to have a decent chance to scale the walls and achieve what they wished. Wealth, rank, or an imposing name counted for nothing. The only credential the city asked was the boldness to dream."

As the boy ducked into a tailor shop, Hart recognized that this narrative was not exclusive to his "wonderful city"—it was one that could happen anywhere in, and only in, America. "A surge of shamefaced patriotism overwhelmed me," Hart wrote in his memoir, *Act One.* "I might have been watching a victory parade on a flag-draped Fifth Avenue instead of the mean streets of a city slum. A feeling of patriotism, however, is not always limited to the feverish emotions called forth by war. It can sometimes be felt as profoundly and perhaps more truly at a moment such as this."

Hart, like so many before and after him, was overcome by the power of the American Dream. As a people, we Americans are unique in having such a thing, a more or less Official National Dream. (There is no correspondingly stirring Canadian Dream or Slovakian Dream.) It is part of our charter—as articulated in the second sentence of the Declaration of Independence, in the famous bit about "certain unalienable Rights" that include "Life, Liberty and the pursuit of Happiness"—and it is what makes our country and our way of life attractive and magnetic to people in other lands.

But now fast-forward to the year 2009, the final Friday of January. The new president is surveying the dire economy he has been charged with righting—600,000 jobs lost in January alone, a gross domestic product that shrank 3.8 percent in the final quarter of 2008, the worst contraction in almost 30 years. Assessing these numbers, Barack Obama, a man who normally exudes hopefulness for a living, pronounces them a "continuing disaster for America's working families," a disaster that amounts to no less, he says, than "the American Dream in reverse."

In reverse. Imagine this in terms of Hart's life: out of the taxicab, back on the subway, back to the tenements, back to cramped cohabitation with Mom and Dad, back to gray mornings and the grim smell of actual want.

You probably don't even have to imagine, for chances are that of late you have experienced some degree of reversal yourself, or at the very least have had friends or loved ones get laid off, lose their homes, or just find themselves forced to give up certain perks and amenities (restaurant meals, cable TV, salon haircuts) that were taken for granted as recently as a year ago.

These are tough times for the American Dream. As the safe routines of our lives have come undone, so has our characteristic optimism—not only our belief that the future is full of limitless possibility, but our faith that things will eventually return to normal, whatever "normal" was before the recession hit. There is even worry that the dream may be over—that we currently living Americans are the unfortunate ones who shall bear witness to that deflating moment in history when the promise of this country began to wither. This is the "sapping of confidence" that President Obama alluded to in his inaugural address, the "nagging fear that America's decline is inevitable, and that the next generation must lower its sights."

But let's face it: If Moss Hart, like so many others, was able to rally from the depths of the Great Depression, then surely the viability of the American Dream isn't in question. What needs to change is our expectation of what the dream promises—and our understanding of what that vague and promiscuously used term, "the American Dream," is really supposed to mean.

In recent years, the term has often been interpreted to mean "making it big" or "striking it rich." (As the cult of Brian De Palma's *Scarface* has grown, so, disturbingly, has the number of people with a literal, celebratory read on its tagline: "He loved the American Dream. With a vengeance.") Even when the phrase isn't being used to describe the accumulation of great wealth, it's frequently deployed to denote extreme success of some kind or other. Last year, I heard commentators say that Barack Obama achieved the American Dream by getting elected president, and that Philadelphia Phillies manager Charlie Manuel achieved the American Dream by leading his team to its first World Series title since 1980.

Yet there was never any promise or intimation of extreme success in the book that popularized the term, *The Epic of America,* by James Truslow Adams, published by Little, Brown and Company in 1931. (Yes, "the American Dream" is a surprisingly recent coinage; you'd think that these words would appear in the writings of

Thomas Jefferson or Benjamin Franklin, but they don't.) For a book that has made such a lasting contribution to our vocabulary, *The Epic of America* is an offbeat piece of work—a sweeping, essayistic, highly subjective survey of this country's development from Columbus's landfall onward, written by a respected but solemn historian whose prim prose style was mocked as "spinach" by the waggish theater critic Alexander Woollcott.

But it's a smart, thoughtful treatise. Adams's goal wasn't so much to put together a proper history of the U.S. as to determine, by tracing his country's path to prominence, what makes this land so unlike other nations, so uniquely *American*. (That he undertook such an enterprise when he did, in the same grim climate in which Hart wrote *Once in a Lifetime,* reinforces how indomitably strong Americans' faith in their country remained during the Depression.) What Adams came up with was a construct he called "that American dream of a better, richer, and happier life for all our citizens of every rank."

From the get-go, Adams emphasized the egalitarian nature of this dream. It started to take shape, he said, with the Puritans who fled religious persecution in England and settled New England in the 17th century. "[Their] migration was not like so many earlier ones in history, led by warrior lords with followers dependent on them," he wrote, "but was one in which the common man as well as the leader was hoping for greater freedom and happiness for himself and his children."

The Declaration of Independence took this concept even further, for it compelled the well-to-do upper classes to put the common man on an equal footing with them where human rights and self-governance were concerned—a nose-holding concession that Adams captured with exquisite comic passiveness in the sentence, "It had been found necessary to base the [Declaration's] argument at last squarely on the rights of man." Whereas the colonist upper classes were asserting their independence from the British Empire, "the lower classes were thinking not only of that," Adams wrote, "but of their relations to their colonial legislatures and governing class."

America was truly a new world, a place where one could live one's life and pursue one's goals unburdened by older societies' prescribed ideas of class, caste, and social hierarchy. Adams was unreserved in his wonderment over this fact. Breaking from his formal tone, he shifted into first-person mode in *The Epic of America's* epilogue, noting a French guest's remark that his most striking impression of the United States was "the way that everyone of every sort looks you right in the eye, without a thought of inequality." Adams also told a story of "a foreigner" he used to employ as an assistant, and how he and this foreigner fell into a habit of chitchatting for a bit after their day's work was done. "Such a relationship was the great difference between America and his homeland," Adams wrote. "There, he said, 'I would do my work and might get a pleasant word, but I could never sit and talk like this. There is a difference there between social grades which cannot be got over. I would not talk to you there as man to man, but as my employer.'"

Anecdotal as these examples are, they get to the crux of the American Dream as Adams saw it: that life in the United States offered personal liberties and opportunities to a degree unmatched by any other country in history—a circumstance that remains true today, some ill-considered clampdowns in the name of Homeland Security notwithstanding. This invigorating sense of possibility, though it is too often taken for granted, is the great gift of Americanness. Even Adams underestimated it. Not above the prejudices of his time, he certainly never saw Barack Obama's presidency coming. While he correctly anticipated the eventual assimilation of the millions of Eastern and Southern European immigrants who arrived in the early 20th century to work in America's factories, mines, and sweatshops, he entertained no such hopes for black people. Or, as he rather injudiciously put it, "After a generation or two, [the white-ethnic laborers] can be absorbed, whereas the negro cannot."

It's also worth noting that Adams did not deny that there is a material component to the American Dream. *The Epic of America* offers several variations on Adams's definition of the dream (e.g., "the American dream that life should be made richer and fuller for everyone and opportunity remain open to all"), but the word "richer" appears in all of them, and he wasn't just talking about richness of experience. Yet Adams was careful not to overstate what the dream promises. In one of his final iterations of the "American Dream" trope, he described it as "that dream of a land in which life should be better and richer and fuller for every man, with opportunity for each according to his ability or achievement."

That last part—"according to his ability or achievement"—is the tempering phrase, a shrewd bit of expectations management. A "better and richer life" is promised, but for most people this won't be a rich person's life. "Opportunity for each" is promised, but within the bounds of each person's ability; the reality is, some people will realize the American Dream more stupendously and significantly than others. (For example, while President Obama is correct in saying, "Only in America is my story possible," this does not make it true that anyone in America can be the next Obama.) Nevertheless, the American Dream is within reach for all those who aspire to it and are willing to put in the hours; Adams was articulating it as an attainable outcome, not as a pipe dream.

As the phrase "the American Dream" insinuated its way into the lexicon, its meaning continuously morphed and shifted, reflecting the hopes and wants of the day. Adams, in *The Epic of America*, noted that one such major shift had already occurred in the republic's history, before he'd given the dream its name. In 1890, the U.S. Census Bureau declared that there was no longer such a thing as the American frontier. This was not an official pronouncement but an observation in the bureau's report that "the unsettled area has been so broken into by isolated bodies of settlement that there can hardly be said to be a frontier line."

The tapering off of the frontier era put an end to the immature, individualistic, Wild West version of the American Dream, the one that had animated homesteaders, prospectors, wildcatters, and railroad men. "For a century and more," Adams wrote, "our successive 'Wests' had dominated the thoughts of the poor, the restless, the discontented, the ambitious, as they had those of business expansionists and statesmen."

But by the time Woodrow Wilson became president, in 1913—after the first national election in which every voter in the continental U.S. cast his ballot as a citizen of an established state—that vision had become passé. In fact, to hear the new president speak, the frontiersman's version of the American Dream was borderline malevolent. Speaking in his inaugural address as if he had just attended a screening of *There Will Be Blood*, Wilson declared, "We have squandered a great part of what we might have used, and have not stopped to conserve the exceeding bounty of nature, without which our genius for enterprise would have been worthless and impotent." Referencing both the end of the frontier and the rapid industrialization that arose in its aftermath, Wilson said, "There has been something crude and heartless and unfeeling in our haste to succeed and be great.... We have come now to the sober second thought. The scales of heedlessness have fallen from our eyes. We have made up our minds to square every process of our national life again with the standards we so proudly set up at the beginning."

The American Dream was maturing into a shared dream, a societal compact that reached its apotheosis when Franklin Delano Roosevelt was sworn into office in 1933 and began implementing the New Deal. A "better and richer and fuller" life was no longer just what America promised its hardworking citizens individually; it was an ideal toward which these citizens were duty-bound to strive together.

**We're still fortunate to live in a country that offers us such latitude in choosing how we go about our lives and work.**

The Social Security Act of 1935 put this theory into practice. It mandated that workers and their employers contribute, via payroll taxes, to federally administered trust funds that paid out benefits to retirees—thereby introducing the idea of a "safe old age" with built-in protection from penury.

This was, arguably, the first time that a specific material component was ascribed to the American Dream, in the form of a guarantee that you could retire at the age of 65 and rest assured that your fellow citizens had your back. On January 31, 1940, a hardy Vermonter named Ida May Fuller, a former legal secretary, became the very first retiree to receive a monthly Social Security benefit check, which totaled $22.54. As if to prove both the best hopes of Social Security's proponents and the worst fears of its detractors, Fuller enjoyed a long retirement, collecting benefits all the way to her death in 1975, when she was 100 years old.

Still, the American Dream, in F.D.R.'s day, remained largely a set of deeply held ideals rather than a checklist of goals or entitlements. When Henry Luce published his famous essay "The American Century" in *Life* magazine in February 1941, he urged that the U.S. should no longer remain on the sidelines of World War II but use its might to promote this country's "love of freedom, a feeling for the equality of opportunity, a tradition of self-reliance and independence, and also of cooperation." Luce was essentially proposing that the American Dream—more or less as Adams had articulated it—serve as a global advertisement for our way of life, one to which non-democracies should be converted, whether by force or gentle coercion. (He was a missionary's son.)

More soberly and less bombastically, Roosevelt, in his 1941 State of the Union address, prepared America for war by articulating the "four essential human freedoms" that the U.S. would be fighting for: "freedom of speech and expression"; "freedom of every person to worship God in his own way"; "freedom from want"; and "freedom from fear." Like Luce, Roosevelt was upholding the American way as a model for other nations to follow—he suffixed each of these freedoms with the phrase "everywhere in the world"—but he presented the four freedoms not as the lofty principles of a benevolent super race but as the homespun, bedrock values of a good, hardworking, unextravagant people.

No one grasped this better than Norman Rockwell, who, stirred to action by Roosevelt's speech, set to work on his famous "Four Freedoms" paintings: the one with the rough-hewn workman speaking his piece at a town meeting (*Freedom of Speech*); the one with the old lady praying in the pew (*Freedom of Worship*); the one with the Thanksgiving dinner (*Freedom from Want*); and the one with the young parents looking in on their sleeping children (*Freedom from Fear*). These paintings, first reproduced in the *Saturday Evening Post* in 1943, proved enormously popular, so much so that the original works were commandeered for a national tour that raised $133 million in U.S. war bonds, while the Office of War Information printed up four million poster copies for distribution.

Whatever your opinion of Rockwell (and I'm a fan), the resonance of the "Four Freedoms" paintings with wartime Americans offers tremendous insight into how U.S. citizens viewed their idealized selves. *Freedom from Want*, the most popular of all, is especially telling, for the scene it depicts is joyous but defiantly unostentatious. There is a happily gathered family, there are plain white curtains, there is a large turkey, there are some celery stalks in a dish, and there is a bowl of fruit, but there is not a hint of overabundance, overindulgence, elaborate table settings, ambitious seasonal centerpieces, or any other conventions of modern-day shelter-mag porn.

It was freedom from want, not freedom to want—a world away from the idea that the patriotic thing to do in tough times is go shopping. Though the germ of that idea would form shortly, not long after the war ended.

William J. Levitt was a Seabee in the Pacific theater during the war, a member of one of the Construction Battalions (CBs) of the U.S. Navy. One of his jobs was to build airfields at as fast a clip as possible, on the cheap. Levitt had already worked in his father's construction business back home, and he held an option on a thousand acres of potato fields in Hempstead, New York, out on Long Island. Coming back from the war with newly acquired speed-building skills and a vision of all those returning G.I.'s needing homes, he set to work on turning those potato fields into the first Levittown.

Levitt had the forces of history and demographics on his side. The G.I. Bill, enacted in 1944, at the tail end of the New Deal, offered returning veterans low-interest loans with no money down to purchase a house—an ideal scenario, coupled with a severe housing shortage and a boom in young families, for the rapid-fire development of suburbia.

The first Levitt houses, built in 1947, had two bedrooms, one bathroom, a living room, a kitchen, and an unfinished loft attic that could theoretically be converted into another bedroom. The houses had no basements or garages, but they sat on lots of 60 by 100 feet, and—McMansionistas, take note—took up only 12 percent of their lot's footprint. They cost about $8,000.

"Levittown" is today a byword for creepy suburban conformity, but Bill Levitt, with his Henry Ford–like acumen for mass production, played a crucial role in making home ownership a new tenet of the American Dream, especially as he expanded his operations to other states and inspired imitators. From 1900 to 1940, the percentage of families who lived in homes that they themselves owned held steady at around 45 percent. But by 1950 this figure had shot up to 55 percent, and by 1960 it was at 62 percent. Likewise, the homebuilding business, severely depressed during the war, revived abruptly at war's end, going from 114,000 new single-family houses started in 1944 to 937,000 in 1946—and to 1.7 million in 1950.

Levitt initially sold his houses only to vets, but this policy didn't hold for long; demand for a new home of one's own wasn't remotely limited to ex-G.I.'s, as the Hollywood filmmaker Frank Capra was astute enough to note in *It's a Wonderful Life*. In 1946, a full year before the first Levittown was populated, Capra's creation George Bailey (played by Jimmy Stewart) cut the ribbon on his own eponymous suburban-tract development, Bailey Park, and his first customer wasn't a war veteran but a hardworking Italian immigrant, the tremulously grateful saloonkeeper Mr. Martini. (An overachiever, Capra was both a war veteran and a hardworking Italian immigrant.)

Buttressed by postwar optimism and prosperity, the American Dream was undergoing another recalibration. Now it really did translate into specific goals rather than Adams's more broadly defined aspirations. Home ownership was the fundamental goal, but, depending on who was doing the dreaming, the package might also include car ownership, television ownership (which multiplied from 6 million to 60 million sets in the U.S. between 1950 and 1960), and the intent to send one's kids to college. The G.I. Bill was as crucial on that last count as it was to the housing boom. In providing tuition money for returning vets, it not only stocked the universities with new students—in 1947, roughly half of the nation's college enrollees were ex-G.I.'s—but put the very idea of college within reach of a generation that had previously considered higher education the exclusive province of the rich and the extraordinarily gifted. Between 1940 and 1965, the number of U.S. adults who had completed at least four years of college more than doubled.

Nothing reinforced the seductive pull of the new, suburbanized American Dream more than the burgeoning medium of television, especially as its production nexus shifted from New York, where the grubby, schlubby shows *The Honeymooners* and *The Phil Silvers Show* were shot, to Southern California, where the sprightly, twinkly shows *The Adventures of Ozzie and Harriet, Father Knows Best,* and *Leave It to Beaver* were made. While the former shows are actually more enduringly watchable and funny, the latter were the foremost "family" sitcoms of the 1950s—and, as such, the aspirational touchstones of real American families.

The Nelsons (*Ozzie and Harriet*), the Andersons (*Father Knows Best*), and the Cleavers (*Leave It to Beaver*) lived in airy houses even nicer than those that Bill Levitt built. In fact, the Nelson home in *Ozzie and Harriet* was a faithful replica of the two-story Colonial in Hollywood where Ozzie, Harriet, David, and Ricky Nelson really lived when they weren't filming their show. The Nelsons also offered, in David and especially the swoonsome, guitar-strumming Ricky, two attractive exemplars of that newly ascendant and clout-wielding American demographic, the teenager. "The postwar spread of American values would be spearheaded by the idea of the teenager," writes Jon Savage somewhat ominously in *Teenage*, his history of youth culture. "This new type was pleasure-seeking, product-hungry, embodying the new global society where social inclusion was to be granted through purchasing power."

Still, the American Dream was far from degenerating into the consumerist nightmare it would later become (or, more precisely, become mistaken for). What's striking about the *Ozzie and Harriet*–style 50s dream is its relative modesty of scale. Yes, the TV and advertising portrayals of family life were antiseptic and too-too-perfect, but the dream homes, real and fictional, seem downright dowdy to modern eyes, with none of the "great room" pretensions and tricked-out kitchen islands that were to come.

Nevertheless, some social critics, such as the economist John Kenneth Galbraith, were already fretful. In his 1958 book *The Affluent Society*, a best-seller, Galbraith posited that America had reached an almost unsurpassable and unsustainable degree of mass affluence because the average family owned a home, one car, and one TV. In pursuing these goals, Galbraith said, Americans had lost a sense of their priorities, focusing on consumerism at the expense of public-sector needs like parks, schools, and infrastructure maintenance. At the same time, they had lost their parents' Depression-era sense of thrift, blithely taking out personal loans or enrolling in installment plans to buy their cars and refrigerators.

While these concerns would prove prescient, Galbraith severely underestimated the potential for average U.S. household income and spending power to grow further. The very same year that *The Affluent Society* came out, Bank of America introduced the BankAmericard, the forerunner to Visa, today the most widely used credit card in the world.

What unfolded over the next generation was the greatest standard-of-living upgrade that this country had ever experienced: an economic sea change powered by the middle class's newly sophisticated engagement in personal finance via credit cards, mutual funds, and discount brokerage houses—and its willingness to take on debt.

Consumer credit, which had already rocketed upward from $2.6 billion to $45 billion in the postwar period (1945 to 1960), shot up to $105 billion by 1970. "It was as if the entire middle class was betting that tomorrow would be better than today," as the financial writer Joe Nocera put it in his 1994 book, *A Piece of the Action: How the Middle Class Joined the Money Class*. "Thus did Americans begin to spend money they didn't yet have; thus did the unaffordable become affordable. And thus, it must be said, did the economy grow."

Before it spiraled out of control, the "money revolution," to use Nocera's term for this great middle-class financial engagement, really did serve the American Dream. It helped make life "better and richer and fuller" for a broad swath of the populace in ways that our Depression-era forebears could only have imagined.

To be glib about it, the Brady family's way of life was even sweeter than the Nelson family's. *The Brady Bunch,* which debuted in 1969, in *The Adventures of Ozzie and Harriet*'s old Friday-night-at-eight slot on ABC, occupied the same space in the American psyche of the 70s as *Ozzie and Harriet* had in the 50s: as the middle class's American Dream wish-fulfillment fantasy, again in a generically idyllic Southern California setting. But now there were two cars in the driveway. Now there were annual vacations at the Grand Canyon and an improbably caper-filled trip to Hawaii. (The average number of airplane trips per American household, less than one per year in 1954, was almost three per year in 1970.) And the house itself was snazzier—that open-plan living area just inside the Brady home's entryway, with the "floating" staircase leading up to the bedrooms, was a major step forward in fake-nuclear-family living.

By 1970, for the first time, more than half of all U.S. families held at least one credit card. But usage was still relatively conservative: only 22 percent of cardholders carried a balance from one month's bill to the next. Even in the so-called go-go 80s, this figure hovered in the 30s, compared to 56 percent today. But it was in the 80s that the American Dream began to take on hyperbolic connotations, to be conflated with extreme success: wealth, basically. The representative TV families, whether benignly genteel (the Huxtables on *The Cosby Show*) or soap-opera bonkers (the Carringtons on *Dynasty*), were undeniably rich. "Who says you can't have it all?" went the jingle in a ubiquitous beer commercial from the era, which only got more alarming as it went on to ask, "Who says you can't have the world without losing your soul?"

The deregulatory atmosphere of the Reagan years—the loosening of strictures on banks and energy companies, the reining in of the Justice Department's antitrust division, the removal of vast tracts of land from the Department of the Interior's protected list—was, in a sense, a calculated regression to the immature, individualistic American Dream of yore; not for nothing did Ronald Reagan (and, later, far less effectively, George W. Bush) go out of his way to cultivate a frontiersman's image, riding horses, chopping wood, and reveling in the act of clearing brush.

To some degree, this outlook succeeded in rallying middle-class Americans to seize control of their individual fates as never before—to "Go for it!," as people in yellow ties and red braces were fond of saying at the time. In one of Garry Trudeau's finest moments from the 80s, a *Doonesbury* character was shown watching a political campaign ad in which a woman concluded her pro-Reagan testimonial with the tagline "Ronald Reagan ... because I'm worth it."

But this latest recalibration saw the American Dream get decoupled from any concept of the common good (the movement to privatize Social Security began to take on momentum) and, more portentously, from the concepts of working hard and managing one's expectations. You only had to walk as far as your mailbox to discover that you'd been "pre-approved" for six new credit cards, and that the credit limits on your existing cards had been raised without your even asking. Never before had money been freer, which is to say, never before had taking on debt become so guilt-less and seemingly consequence-free—at both the personal and institutional levels. President Reagan added $1 trillion to the national debt, and in 1986, the United States, formerly the world's biggest creditor nation, became the world's biggest debt-or nation. Perhaps debt was the new frontier.

A curious phenomenon took hold in the 1990s and 2000s. Even as the easy credit continued, and even as a sustained bull market cheered investors and pa-pered over the coming mortgage and credit crises that we now face, Americans were losing faith in the American Dream—or whatever it was they believed the American Dream to be. A CNN poll taken in 2006 found that more than half of those surveyed, 54 percent, considered the American Dream unachievable—and CNN noted that the numbers were nearly the same in a 2003 poll it had conducted. Before that, in 1995, a *Business Week*/Harris poll found that two-thirds of those surveyed believed the American Dream had become harder to achieve in the past 10 years, and three-fourths believed that achieving the dream would be harder still in the upcoming 10 years.

To the writer Gregg Easterbrook, who at the beginning of this decade was a vis-iting fellow in economics at the Brookings Institution, this was all rather puzzling, because, by the definition of any prior American generation, the American Dream had been more fully realized by more people than ever before. While acknowledg-ing that an obscene amount of America's wealth was concentrated in the hands of a small group of ultra-rich, Easterbrook noted that "the bulk of the gains in liv-ing standards—the gains that really matter—have occurred below the plateau of wealth."

By nearly every measurable indicator, Easterbrook pointed out in 2003, life for the average American had gotten better than it used to be. Per capita income, adjusted for inflation, had more than doubled since 1960. Almost 70 percent of Americans owned the places they lived in, versus under 20 percent a century earlier. Furthermore, U.S. citizens averaged 12.3 years of education, tops in the world and a length of time in school once reserved solely for the upper class.

Yet when Easterbrook published these figures in a book, the book was called *The Progress Paradox: How Life Gets Better While People Feel Worse*. He was paying at-tention not only to the polls in which people complained that the American Dream was out of reach, but to academic studies by political scientists and mental-health experts that detected a marked uptick since the midcentury in the number of Amer-icans who considered themselves unhappy.

The American Dream was now almost by definition unattainable, a moving tar-get that eluded people's grasp; nothing was ever enough. It compelled Americans to set unmeetable goals for themselves and then consider themselves failures when these goals, inevitably, went unmet. In examining why people were thinking this way, Easterbrook raised an important point. "For at least a century," he wrote, "Western life has been dominated by a revolution of rising expectations: Each generation expected more than its antecedent. Now most Americans and Europeans already have what they need, in addition to considerable piles of stuff they don't need."

This might explain the existential ennui of the well-off, attractive, solipsistic kids on *Laguna Beach* (2004–6) and *The Hills* (2006–9), the MTV reality soaps that represent the curdling of the whole Southern California wish-fulfillment genre on television. Here were affluent beach-community teens enriching themselves further not even by acting or working in any real sense, but by allowing themselves to be filmed as they sat by campfires maundering on about, like, how much their lives suck.

In the same locale that begat these programs, Orange County, there emerged a Bill Levitt of McMansions, an Iranian-born entrepreneur named Hadi Makarechian whose company, Capital Pacific Holdings, specializes in building tract-housing developments for multi-millionaires, places with names like Saratoga Cove and Ritz Pointe. In a 2001 profile of Makarechian in the *New Yorker,* David Brooks mentioned that the builder had run into zoning restrictions on his latest development, called Oceanfront, that prevented the "entry statement"—the walls that mark the entrance to the development—from being any higher than four feet. Noted Brooks drolly, "The people who are buying homes in Oceanfront are miffed about the small entry statement." Nothing was ever enough.

An extreme example, perhaps, but not misrepresentative of the national mindset. It says a lot about our buying habits and constant need for new, better stuff that Congress and the Federal Communications Commission were utterly comfortable with setting a hard 2009 date for the switchover from analog to digital television broadcasting—pretty much assuming that every American household owns or will soon own a flat-panel digital TV—even though such TVs have been widely available for only five years. (As recently as January 2006, just 20 percent of U.S. households owned a digital television, and the average price point for such a television was still above a thousand dollars.)

In hewing to the misbegotten notion that our standard of living must trend inexorably upward, we entered in the late 90s and early 00s into what might be called the Juiceball Era of the American Dream—a time of steroidally outsize purchasing and artificially inflated numbers. As Easterbrook saw it, it was no longer enough for people to keep up with the Joneses; no, now they had to "call and raise the Joneses."

"Bloated houses," he wrote, "arise from a desire to call-and-raise-the-Joneses—surely not from a belief that a seven-thousand-square-foot house that comes right up against the property setback line would be an ideal place in which to dwell." More ominously and to the point: "To call-and-raise-the-Joneses, Americans increasingly take on debt."

This personal debt, coupled with mounting institutional debt, is what has got us in the hole we're in now. While it remains a laudable proposition for a young couple to secure a low-interest loan for the purchase of their first home, the more recent practice of running up huge credit-card bills to pay for, well, whatever, has come back to haunt us. The amount of outstanding consumer debt in the U.S. has gone up every year since 1958, and up an astonishing 22 percent since 2000 alone. The financial historian and *V.F.* contributor Niall Ferguson reckons that the over-leveraging of America has become especially acute in the last 10 years, with the U.S.'s debt burden, as a proportion of the gross domestic product, "in the region of 355 percent," he says. "So, debt is *three and a half times* the output of the economy. That's some kind of historic maximum."

James Truslow Adams's words remind us that we're still fortunate to live in a country that offers us such latitude in choosing how we go about our lives and work—even in this crapola economy. Still, we need to challenge some of the middle-class orthodoxies that have brought us to this point—not least the notion, widely promulgated throughout popular culture, that the middle class itself is a soul-suffocating dead end.

The middle class is a good place to be, and, optimally, where most Americans will spend their lives if they work hard and don't over-extend themselves financially. On *American Idol*, Simon Cowell has done a great many youngsters a great service by telling them that they're not going to Hollywood and that they should find some other line of work. The American Dream is not fundamentally about stardom or extreme success; in recalibrating our expectations of it, we need to appreciate that it is not an all-or-nothing deal—that it is not, as in hip-hop narratives and in Donald Trump's brain, a stark choice between the penthouse and the streets.

And what about the outmoded proposition that each successive generation in the United States must live better than the one that preceded it? While this idea is still crucial to families struggling in poverty and to immigrants who've arrived here in search of a better life than that they left behind, it's no longer applicable to an American middle class that lives more comfortably than any version that came before it. (Was this not one of the cautionary messages of the most thoughtful movie of 2008, *wall-e*?) I'm no champion of downward mobility, but the time has come to consider the idea of simple continuity: the perpetuation of a contented, sustainable middle-class way of life, where the standard of living remains happily constant from one generation to the next.

This is not a matter of any generation's having to "lower its sights," to use President Obama's words, nor is it a denial that some children of lower- and middle-class parents will, through talent and/or good fortune, strike it rich and bound precipitously into the upper class. Nor is it a moony, nostalgic wish for a return to the scrappy 30s or the suburban 50s, because any sentient person recognizes that there's plenty about the good old days that wasn't so good: the original Social Security program pointedly excluded farmworkers and domestics (i.e., poor rural laborers and minority women), and the original Levittown didn't allow black people in.

But those eras do offer lessons in scale and self-control. The American Dream should require hard work, but it should not require 80-hour workweeks and parents who never see their kids from across the dinner table. The American Dream should entail a first-rate education for every child, but not an education that leaves no extra time for the actual enjoyment of childhood. The American Dream should accommodate the goal of home ownership, but without imposing a lifelong burden of unmeetable debt. Above all, the American Dream should be embraced as the unique sense of possibility that this country gives its citizens—the decent chance, as Moss Hart would say, to scale the walls and achieve what you wish.

## Print Citations

**CMS:** Kamp, David. "Rethinking the American Dream." In *The Reference Shelf: The American Dream*, edited by Annette Calzone, 97-109. Ipswich, MA: H.W. Wilson, 2018.

**MLA:** Kamp, David. "Rethinking the American Dream." *The Reference Shelf: The American Dream*. Ed. Annette Calzone. Ipswich: H.W. Wilson, 2018. 97-109. Print.

**APA:** Kamp, D. (2018). Rethinking the American dream. In Annette Calzone (Ed.), *The reference shelf: The American Dream* (pp. 97-109). Ipswich, MA: H.W. Wilson. (Original work published 2009)

# Is the American Dream Really Dead?

By Carol Graham
*The Guardian*, June 20, 2017

The United States has a long-held reputation for exceptional tolerance of income inequality, explained by its high levels of social mobility. This combination underpins the American dream—initially conceived of by Thomas Jefferson as each citizen's right to the pursuit of life, liberty and the pursuit of happiness.

This dream is not about guaranteed outcomes, of course, but the *pursuit* of opportunities. The dream found a persona in the fictional characters of the 19th-century writer Horatio Alger Jr—in which young working-class protagonists go from rags to riches (or at least become middle class) in part due to entrepreneurial spirit and hard work.

Yet the opportunity to live the American dream is much less widely shared today than it was several decades ago. While 90% of the children born in 1940 ended up in higher ranks of the income distribution than their parents, only 40% of those born in 1980 have done so.

Attitudes about inequality have also changed. In 2001, a study found the only Americans who reported lower levels of happiness amid greater inequality were left-leaning rich people—with the poor seeing inequality as a sign of future opportunity. Such optimism has since been substantially tempered: in 2016, only 38% of Americans thought their children would be better off than they are.

In the meantime, the public discussion about inequality has completely by-passed a critical element of the American dream: luck.

Just as in many of Alger's stories the main character benefits from the assistance of a generous philanthropist, there are countless real examples of success in the US where different forms of luck have played a major role. And yet, social support for the unlucky—in particular, the poor who cannot stay in full-time employment—has been falling substantially in recent years, and is facing even more threats today.

In short, from new research based on some novel metrics of wellbeing, I find strong evidence that the American dream is in tatters, at least.

## White Despair, Minority Hope

My research began by comparing mobility attitudes in the US with those in Latin America, a region long known for high levels of poverty and inequality (although with progress in the past decades). I explored a question in the Gallup world poll, which asks respondents a classic American dream question: "Can an individual who works hard in this country get ahead?"

I found very large gaps between the responses of "the rich" and "the poor" in the US (represented by the top and bottom 20% income distributions of the Gallup respondents). This was in stark contrast to Latin America, where there was no significant difference in attitudes across income groups. Poor people in the US were 20 times less likely to believe hard work would get them ahead than were the poor in Latin America, even though the latter are significantly worse off in material terms.

Another question in the poll explores whether or not respondents experience stress on a daily basis. Stress is a marker of poor health, and the kind of stress typically experienced by the poor—usually due to negative shocks that are beyond their control ("bad stress") —is significantly worse for wellbeing than "good stress": that which is associated with goal achievement, for those who feel able to focus on their future.

In general, Latin Americans experience significantly less stress—and also smile more—on a daily basis than Americans. The gaps between the poor and rich in the US were significantly wider (by 1.5 times on a 0–1 score) than those in Latin America, with the poor in the US experiencing more stress than either the rich or poor in Latin America.

The gaps between the expectations and sentiments of rich and poor in the US are also greater than in many other countries in east Asia and Europe (the other regions studied). It seems that being poor in a very wealthy and unequal country—which prides itself on being a meritocracy, and eschews social support for those who fall behind—results in especially high levels of stress and desperation.

But my research also yielded some surprises. With the low levels of belief in the value of hard work and high levels of stress among poor respondents in the US as a starting point, I compared optimism about the future across poor respondents of different races. This was based on a question

**In 2016, only 38% of Americans thought their children would be better off than they are.**

in the US Gallup daily poll that asks respondents where they think they will be five years from now on a 0-10 step life satisfaction ladder.

I found that poor minorities—and particularly black people—were much more optimistic about the future than poor white people. Indeed, poor black respondents were three times as likely to be a point higher up on the optimism ladder than were poor whites, while poor Hispanic people were one and a half times more optimistic than whites. Poor black people were also half as likely as poor whites to experience stress the previous day, while poor Hispanics were only two-thirds as likely as poor whites.

What explains the higher levels of optimism among minorities, who have traditionally faced discrimination and associated challenges? There is no simple answer.

One factor is that poor minorities have stronger informal safety nets and social support, such as families and churches, than do their white counterparts.

Psychologists also find that minorities are more resilient and much less likely to report depression or commit suicide than are whites in the face of negative shocks, perhaps due to a longer trajectory of dealing with negative shocks and challenges.

Another critical issue is the threat and reality of downward mobility for blue-collar whites, particularly in the heartland of the country where manufacturing, mining, and other jobs have hollowed out. Andrew Cherlin of Johns Hopkins University finds that poor black and Hispanic people are much more likely than poor white people to report that they live better than their parents did. Poor whites are more likely to say they live worse than their parents did; they, in particular, seem to be living the erosion of the American dream.

## The American Problem

Why does this matter? My research from a decade ago—since confirmed by other studies—found that individuals who were optimistic about their futures tended to have better health and employment outcomes. Those who believe in their futures tend to invest in those futures, while those who are consumed with stress, daily struggles and a lack of hope, not only have less means to make such investments, but also have much less confidence that they will pay off.

The starkest marker of lack of hope in the US is a significant increase in premature mortality in the past decade—driven by an increase in suicides and drug and alcohol poisoning and a stalling of progress against heart disease and lung cancer—primarily but not only among middle-aged uneducated white people. Mortality rates for black and Hispanic people, while higher on average than those for whites, continued to fall during the same time period.

The reasons for this trend are multi-faceted. One is the coincidence of an all-too-readily-available supply of drugs such as opioids, heroin and fentanyl, with the shrinking of blue-collar jobs—and identities—primarily due to technological change. Fifteen per cent of prime age males are out of the labour force today; with that figure projected to increase to 25% by 2050. The identity of the blue-collar worker seems to be stronger for white people than for minorities, meanwhile. While there are now increased employment opportunities in services such as health, white males are far less likely to take them up than are their minority counterparts.

Lack of hope also contributes to rising mortality rates, as evidenced in my latest research with Sergio Pinto. On average, individuals with lower optimism for the future are more likely to live in metropolitan statistical areas (MSAs) with higher mortality rates for 45- to 54-year-olds.

Desperate people are more likely to die prematurely, but living with a lot of premature death can also erode hope. Higher average levels of optimism in metropolitan areas are also associated with lower premature mortality rates. These same places tend to be more racially diverse, healthier (as gauged by fewer respondents who smoke and more who exercise), and more likely to be urban and economically vibrant.

Technology-driven growth is not unique to the US, and low-skilled workers face challenges in many OECD countries. Yet by contrast, away from the US, they have not had a similar increase in premature mortality. One reason may be stronger social welfare systems—and stronger norms of collective social responsibility for those who fall behind—in Europe.

Ironically, part of the problem may actually *be* the American dream. Blue-collar white people—whose parents lived the American dream and who expected their children to do so as well—are the ones who seem most devastated by its erosion and yet, on average, tend to vote against government programmes. In contrast, minorities, who have been struggling for years and have more experience multi-tasking on the employment front and relying on family and community support when needed—are more resilient and hopeful, precisely because they still see a chance for moving up the ladder.

There are high costs to being poor in America, where winners win big but losers fall hard. Indeed, the dream, with its focus on individual initiative in a meritocracy, has resulted in far less public support than there is in other countries for safety nets, vocational training, and community support for those with disadvantage or bad luck. Such strategies are woefully necessary now, particularly in the heartland where some of Alger's characters might have come from, but their kind have long since run out of luck.

## Print Citations

**CMS:** Graham, Carol. "Is the American Dream Really Dead?" In *The Reference Shelf: The American Dream,* edited by Annette Calzone, 110-113. Ipswich, MA: H.W. Wilson, 2018.

**MLA:** Graham, Carol. "Is the American Dream Really Dead?" *The Reference Shelf: The American Dream.* Ed. Annette Calzone. Ipswich: H.W. Wilson, 2018. 110-113. Print.

**APA:** Graham, C. (2018). Is the American dream really dead? In Annette Calzone (Ed.), *The reference shelf: The American Dream* (pp. 110-113). Ipswich, MA: H.W. Wilson. (Original work published 2017)

# American "Exceptionalism" Is Holding America Back from Greatness

## By Alasdair S. Roberts
*Quartz*, March 21, 2018

Exceptionalism—the idea that the United States has a mission and character that separates it from other nations—is ingrained in everyday talk about American politics.

It shapes high-level discussions about foreign policy—for example, in a recent argument by a foreign affairs scholar that the United States plays a "unique role as the world's anchor of liberal ideas."

It shapes conversation about domestic policy too. It leads us to think that America's internal divisions and problems are distinctive—and by implication, that the experience of other countries cannot tell us much about how to handle them.

But is the United States really exceptional?

## Every Country Is Special

It is, at a basic level, of course. Every country believes that its circumstances are distinctive. Russians talk about their "specialness." The Chinese insist on their "uniqueness." Indians have long noted the unusual complexity of their politics.

Beyond this, though, the idea of American exceptionalism does not hold up. My research suggests that it is also obstructing the country's ability to think clearly about the challenges ahead.

Exceptionalism has two aspects. One is the notion that the United States, since its founding, has had a distinct ambition—a "messianic mission" to promote liberty and democracy.

By itself, having a national mission is not unusual. The European empires of the 19th century were also driven by grand ambitions. The French talked about their mission to civilize the world. The British promoted "British ideals" such as liberty and the rule of law. They even promised eventual self-government for colonies—when London judged that the colonies were ready for it.

The American practice was not entirely different. The country's leaders declared their mission to civilize the continent. They acquired territory, often by force, and then decided whether people were ready to govern themselves. The empowerment of African-Americans, Hispanic-Americans, native peoples, and immigrants was delayed because they were considered by the white An-glo-Saxon majority to be "ill-fitted for self-rule."

> **Rhetoric about US exceptionalism does not help to build alliances.**

And the United States was also a colonizing power. For example, it occupied the Philippines in the first half of the 20th century, sought to introduce "American civilization," and again deferred self-rule because Filipinos were judged not to be ready for it.

In the 20th century, politicians in the United States and Europe were pushed toward a more enlightened view of freedom. Faced with protests and rebellions, Western countries gave up most of their colonies and enfranchised more of their people. And they adopted codes like the Universal Declaration of Human Rights and the European Convention on Human Rights.

## Freedom and Democracy, a Shared Goal

Again, though, the United States was not exceptional in its pursuit of freedom and democracy. There was a shared commitment to human rights, even though countries often fell short of the ideal in practice.

This claim does not get the scrutiny it deserves. Sometimes it relies on a stereotype of centralized government in Europe. It overlooks Europe's long history of uprisings, civil wars, coups, and partitions. Deep ambivalence about authority is certainly not peculiar to the United States. The second aspect of exceptionalism has to do with the character of American society and politics. The claim is that governing in the United States is different than in Europe because the US population is so diverse, people are so wedded to their rights, and central government has been historically weak. After all, the United States was born in revolution. And it empowered the people before modern conditions required strong government.

Moreover, western Europe accounts for a small minority of the world's 195 states. Almost half of those states are fewer than 80 years old. Most are categorized as fragile. Leaders in fragile states struggle to establish central authority and manage deep internal divisions, while respecting domestic and international law on human rights.

In short, they wrestle with all of the challenges that are said to make the United States exceptional.

## Need to Recognize Commonalities

This wrongheaded emphasis on exceptionalism is unfortunate for two reasons.

The first is that it complicates the task of building a global coalition to defend freedom and democracy. Recent history shows the urgent need for such a coalition. Around the world, democracy is perceived to be in retreat. China, a one-party state, will soon have the world's biggest economy. In the fight to advance human rights, the United States needs all the friends it can get. Rhetoric about US exceptionalism does not help to build alliances.

It also undermines the country's capacity to deal with one of the most challenging aspects of democratic governance. This is the problem of managing sharp internal divisions without resorting to methods that crush liberties and respect for minorities.

As any history book will show, the United States has much experience with this problem. But so do many other countries. Some, like India, the world's most populous liberal democracy, deal with it on a much larger scale. There is an opportunity to learn across borders. Rhetoric about exceptionalism makes it less likely that this will happen.

In this century, the pursuit of traditional American ideals requires new ways of thinking. The ambition to advance freedom and democracy is now broadly shared. So is experience in translating these ideals into practice. To defend those ideals, all of the world's democracies must pull together in a common cause.

The first step is adopting a new point of view. Call it unexceptionalism: an attitude that acknowledges the commonalities, as well as the differences, in the American experience.

## Print Citations

**CMS:** Roberts, Alasdair S. "American 'Exceptionalism' Is Holding America Back from Greatness." In *The Reference Shelf: The American Dream,* edited by Annette Calzone, 114-116. Ipswich, MA: H.W. Wilson, 2018.

**MLA:** Roberts, Alasdair S. "American 'Exceptionalism' Is Holding America Back from Greatness." *The Reference Shelf: The American Dream.* Ed. Annette Calzone. Ipswich: H.W. Wilson, 2018. 114-116. Print.

**APA:** Roberts, A.S. (2018). American "exceptionalism" is holding America back from greatness. In Annette Calzone (Ed.), *The reference shelf: The American Dream* (pp. 114-116). Ipswich, MA: H.W. Wilson. (Original work published 2018)

# 5
# Future of the Dream

The American Dream will change once again when new technologies become part of the economic landscape. Will artificial intelligence create more jobs than it destroys? Will the United States be a leader in tech development? Here, people view a model T60 drone made by the Chinese firm JTT during the International Drone Expo in Los Angeles, CA, on December 10, 2016.

# The Future of the American Dream

Economists and social scientists have explored how the American dream is changing, but the future of the dream remains unclear. Some economists and political scientists are concerned that the rapid development of technology is a threat to the dream, driving the labor market into disarray much as industrialization did in the nineteenth and twentieth centuries. In the political realm, economists and social scientists have expressed concern that America is losing its edge in innovation and development, with economic competitors like China increasingly playing a dominant role in the development of new products. These and other challenges are the subject of research and political debate as Americans struggle to realize their own success in the modern world and to ensure that future generations can also secure some portion of an American dream.

## Technology and Innovation

Increasingly, social scientists and tech experts are becoming divided into camps over the issue of whether the increasing integration of advanced technology will be good or bad for the American labor market. Some see emerging technology like artificial intelligence (AI) as a potential boon, creating new jobs and driving rapid economic growth. Others fear a darker future, with technology disrupting the entire labor market and leading to potentially disastrous job losses.

Those who feel that rising tech integration will be bad for the economy have several prominent studies by economic forecasters as evidence. For instance, a July 2016 study released by *McKinsey Quarterly* found that nearly 45 percent of jobs currently handled by people could be automated simply with current levels of technology. This includes everything from repetitive physical tasks and data processing to 20 percent of the work currently handled by chief executive officers (CEOs) in American corporations. This estimate is conservative as well, as new developments in AI and machine learning mean that automation could eventually impact jobs in fields today considered "safe" from replacement. Researchers at *McKinsey* suggest that as many as 400 to 800 million jobs worldwide could be automated by 2030, with tens of millions potentially out of work around the world.[1]

On the other side of the debate, technological optimists argue that technology like AI will create more jobs than it destroys. The Gartner research group, for instance, predicted that AI would eliminate 1.8 million U.S. jobs by 2020, but would create 2.3 million jobs in that same period. Whether automation harms or helps humanity, say technological optimists, will depend on how society reacts to this encroaching technology. For instance, though the advent of "chatbots" (machines designed to carry out a conversation with a human) eliminated thousands of jobs around the world, supporters argue that chatbots eliminate mundane and routine tasks and free humans for more worthwhile tasks.[2] Further, supporters of the technological revolution argue that technology increases leisure time for workers, and in many cases, increases pay and thus creates additional spending capital that creates new jobs in services. A report from the Society of Business Economists in England looked at how technology affected the job market during the industrial revolution and found that while in 1871 only 1.1 percent of British citizens worked in service positions, with 23.7 percent employed in manual labor, by 2011, 12.2 percent worked in services, with 8.3 percent still employed in labor positions. As factory jobs replaced agricultural jobs, there was an increased demand for recreation, grooming, and leisure, leading to a vast increase in the number of bars, restaurants, hairdressers, and other services once seen as luxuries only for the wealthy.[3]

Historians frequently look at the industrial revolution for clues as to how America's current technological revolution may impact society. As the United Kingdom study discussed above found, over 140 years, job gains from the industrial revolution vastly exceeded job losses, though this process took considerable time. In the United Kingdom and the United States, the industrial revolution marked a major shift in the basic patterns of human life, a transition from a predominantly agricultural culture to one of urban life and industrial production. In the United States, the industrial revolution occurred alongside the Golden Age of Immigration in which tens of millions of immigrants came to the United States to work in the nation's cities and factories. This fueled the rapid growth of the American economy and cemented the United States as one of the world's economic superpowers. Americans have, in a sense, never lost their enthusiasm for technological innovation, having culturally embraced the idea that technology has been key to the success of the United States on the world stage.

However, the transition from agriculture to industry came at a serious human cost as tens of thousands lost their jobs and were made obsolete by the march of technology. This now largely forgotten transition is sometimes disregarded in histories and described as a labor market "adjustment." Consider, for instance, that the advent of the automobile created dozens of cutting-edge jobs to the labor market, including automotive mechanics, manufacturers, drivers, and machinists. However, the automobile and railroad devastated the horse-powered transport and shipping industries that had existed for a century before. This meant a loss of livelihood for horse breeders and trainers, drivers of carts, caravans, and other horse-powered conveyances, farriers (people who shoe horses), blacksmiths, saddle and horse-equipment manufacturers, and many others. While the industrial revolution therefore created new, innovative jobs, and ultimately increased the affluence of American culture, this came after decades of displacement and turmoil. Technological skeptics today ask whether the societies of the world can withstand another such period waiting for the labor market to adjust.[4]

The American dream is about prosperity, or at least, about the potential for advancement and about living in a society that is supposed to facilitate that process. At the base of this dream is the capability to obtain an education and a sustainable job. Given the current crises regarding economic inequality, the erosion of the middle class, and wage stagnation, the United States already faces significant hurdles to fostering sustainable lives and careers for its citizens and so it is unclear whether or not the nation can or will be able to find any way to help citizens adjust to further technological disruption.

If governments fail to control the tendency for businesses in the private market to prioritize profit over human concerns, the changes that society is experiencing will likely lead to widespread unemployment and deepening poverty until the labor market adjusts to these changes. If governments make human interest their chief priority, managing and limiting the implementation of technology that will cause job losses, society may be able to help guide humanity toward a more productive future working with technological tools.

## Innovating the American Dream

Innovation is a characteristic that many Americans would likely ascribe to their nation. In terms of popular culture alone, the United States has proven innovative enough to drive global trends for decades, and in the twentieth century, the United States was a global leader in the development of new technologies. Sometimes this innovation comes from careful, measured investment. The National Aeronautics and Space Administration (NASA), for instance, was created through decades of governmental investment culminating in America becoming the global leader in space exploration into the modern era. At other times, American inventiveness springs up by accident, like the invention of the microwave oven, which occurred when military researcher Percy Spencer was testing a magnetron device and realized that he had accidentally melted his snack. Whether by fortune or foresight, America's innovativeness has always kept the nation ahead of the curve when it came to the development of new ideas and technology. The internet, now a backbone of global commerce, reached its potential through American research and development.

Increasingly, however, some economists and politicians have become concerned that the United States is falling behind in terms of innovation. After years of trailing significantly behind the United States, China is rising in international prominence. In 2016, Chinese scientists published more research papers than U.S. scientists for the first time in history.[5]

More optimistic industry analysts argue that there is, as yet, no reason for serious concern. The United States still leads the world in funding for science and still hosts many of the world's leading centers for research. However, while the United States might currently maintain its position as the world's leading investor in scientific research, investing in research alone is not sufficient to guarantee the nation's position as one of the world's leading innovators. The United States has not invested in the development of green and alternative technology, arguably the most important technological trend of the current age. By failing to invest aggressively in alternative technology, the United States is forfeiting its potential place as an innovator in one of the fastest-growing industrial markets of the century.

The United States achieved global dominance in scientific research not only by investing in but also by identifying and focusing on cutting-edge fields. The question is, can the United States maintain its scientific edge if the nation's internal conflicts prevent the kind of investment needed not only for innovation, but for the kind of innovation that the world currently needs?

## Works Used

Allen, Katie. "Technology Has Created More Jobs Than It Has Destroyed, Says 140 Years of Data." *The Guardian*. The Guardian News and Media. Aug 18, 2015. Retrieved from https://www.theguardian.com/business/2015/aug/17/technology-created-more-jobs-than-destroyed-140-years-data-census.

Chui, Michael, Manyika, James, and Mehdi Miremadi. "Where Machines Could Replace Humans—and Where They Can't (Yet)." *McKinsey Quarterly*. July 2016. Retrieved from https://www.mckinsey.com/business-functions/digital-mckinsey/our-insights/where-machines-could-replace-humans-and-where-they-cant-yet.

Guarino, Ben, Rauhala, Emily, and William Wan. "China Increasingly Challenges American Dominance of Science." *The Washington Post*. The Washington Post Co. Jun 3, 2018. Retrieved from https://www.washingtonpost.com/national/health-science/china-challenges-american-dominance-of-science/2018/06/03/c1e0cfe4-48d5-11e8-827e-190efaf1f1ee_story.html?noredirect=on&utm_term=.8936e99e0226.

Hess, Edward D. "Will Business Leaders Save the American Dream?" *Medium*. Medium. Retrieved from https://medium.com/@edhess33/will-business-leaders-save-the-american-dream-e4d50380d2b.

Roe, David. "Why Artificial Intelligence Will Create More Jobs Than It Destroys." *CMS Wire*. Simpler Media Group, Inc. Jan 9, 2018. Retrieved from https://www.cmswire.com/digital-workplace/why-artificial-intelligence-will-create-more-jobs-than-it-destroys/.

## Notes

1.  Chui, Manyika, and Miremadi, "Where Machines Could Replace Humans—and Where They Can't (Yet)."
2.  Roe, "Why Artificial Intelligence Will Create More Jobs Than It Destroys."
3.  Allen, "Technology Has Created More Jobs Than It Has Destroyed, Says 140 Years of Data."
4.  Hess, "Will Business Leaders Save the American Dream?"
5.  Guarino, Rauhala, and Wan, "China Increasingly Challenges American Dominance of Science."

# Technology: Killer or Savior of the American Dream?

By Frida Polli
*Forbes*, October 12, 2017

The American Dream is fading. Extensive research points to increasing social inequality and grossly declining rates of social mobility.

Technology has been cast as the antagonist to this, the primary killer of the American Dream and perpetuator of social inequality. However, technology itself is neutral; the effects of technology are an embodiment of the humans who create it, manifesting their intentions through their design and implementation of technology's power. Technologies like artificial intelligence have as much potential to create social mobility as they do to further the inequalities facing underprivileged and disenfranchised communities. The directional power of technology is really all in its design.

In reality, the perpetuation of inequality does not stem from AI, but from unchecked elitism preventing mobility into the jobs of the future—something that AI can actually help solve.

Elitism is one of the few (if not the only remaining) "isms" that is actually celebrated today. I have overheard recruiting and business leaders at prestigious companies say that they have no need to expand their efforts beyond elite schools because they are already inundated by these "elite" candidates. A head of diversity recruiting once told me in economic terms what she would be willing to spend on recruiting a "non-elite" student: $5,000 dollars of her recruiting budget compared to the $50,00-100,000 she typically spends recruiting "elite" students. It seemed strangely un-empathetic for someone who was charged with improving all types of diversity. Unfortunately, she is not unique in her point of view.

Now, if elite schools were true meritocracies, then maybe we could justify this attitude. If they really did accept people regardless of their race, gender and socioeconomic background, then we might find this attitude understandable. However, while these institutions have made great strides in terms of gender and ethnic equality, they have largely ignored socioeconomic inequality. As Obama famously said, his children face better odds getting into an elite school than a working-class white person's children.

Looking at Harvard students born between 1981 and 1991, 70% of students came from the top 20% of income distribution, versus 3.5% from the bottom 20%.

Another way to look at it: students from the top 10% of the population outnumbered those from the bottom 90% and as many students came from the infamous 1% as did the bottom 60% (Raj Chetty, Stanford). This was true of 38 schools in the US, including Dartmouth, Princeton, Yale, Penn and Brown.

Additionally, holding academic ability constant, whites from upper middle class backgrounds were 3 times more likely to be admitted to elite colleges than those from low income backgrounds (Espenshade and Radford, Princeton). Eighty-six percent of African Americans at elite colleges come from middle or upper class backgrounds (Bowen and Bok). And while many factors increased your odds of acceptance at an Ivy league school—being an athlete (28%) or a legacy (20%) for starters—being from the bottom income quartile did not (Bowen, 2005).

This begs the question: if you grow up in a poor or working class family, and you have similar grades and standardized test scores as someone who was born into affluence, shouldn't that advantage you at least as much as being an athlete or legacy?

This leads to a cycle of elitism-driven-inequality: High-achieving students from poor backgrounds often do not apply to selective colleges, and even when they do, they have no advantages to getting in. Companies then focus on these elite schools when hiring, promoting that group's social mobility and access to opportunities. Of the 18M students currently in college, only .4% go to Ivy League schools—versus the 40% who attend community college. This means that the vast majority of people who would benefit most from social mobility have the least access to it, leaving America with a growing economic and opportunity gap.

The good news is that technology can actually provide solutions to overcome some of these challenges to social mobility.

First, we can leverage digital recruiting platforms like WayUp, Handshake, The Muse and others to gain access to a much larger swath of the population than analog on-campus recruiting has allowed in the past. Second, we can use online education platforms like EdX, Coursera, General Assembly, and others to find students who are trained in highly relevant skills, regardless of their formal education. Finally, we must stop relying on resumes that lead us to over-index on elite educations. Thanks to developments in technology, we can instead leverage hiring platforms that rely on bias-free AI and better quality

> **The vast majority of people who would benefit most from social mobility have the least access to it, leaving America with a growing economic and opportunity gap.**

data to identify great talent, irrespective of someone's socioeconomic background. At pymetrics, and other companies like HireVue, we use bias-free AI to promote not just gender and racial equality, but also socioeconomic. By using a combination of these technologies, companies at the forefront of innovation have been able to hire deep into the socioeconomic bench for the first time in their history.

These are the hallmarks of innovative, forward thinking companies. Instead of bemoaning "a war for talent," "a pipeline problem," or "looking for top quality hires" (therefore creating a mindset of artificial scarcity in recruiting), they have taken action. As smart businesspeople, they have looked for more creative ways to find higher quality (and more cost-friendly) alternatives. By diversifying their hiring strategies, these companies are using technology to help bring back the American dream.

## Print Citations

**CMS:** Polli, Frida. "Technology: Killer or Savior of the American Dream?" In *The Reference Shelf: The American Dream*, edited by Annette Calzone, 123-125. Ipswich, MA: H.W. Wilson, 2018.

**MLA:** Polli, Frida. "Technology: Killer or Savior of the American Dream?" *The Reference Shelf: The American Dream*. Ed. Annette Calzone. Ipswich: H.W. Wilson, 2018. 123-125. Print.

**APA:** Polli, F. (2018). Technology: Killer or savior of the American dream? In Annette Calzone (Ed.), *The reference shelf: The American Dream* (pp. 123-125). Ipswich, MA: H.W. Wilson. (Original work published 2017)

# Technology Disrupting the American Dream

By Richard Cohen

*The Washington Post*, January 19, 2015

Mercedes-Benz wants to develop a driverless car. Google already has one. This is exceedingly bad news for auto body shops, ambulance-chasing lawyers and others. Soon, truck drivers might be replaced by driverless trucks. What then will happen to the nation's 3.5 million truck drivers, not to mention truck stops, of which there are 276 in Texas alone? (You can Google anything.)

The conventional answer is retraining. Truck drivers will become something else, maybe teachers or dental hygienists, which is, of course, possible. It's also likely that many of them will sink into the funk that is the loyal companion of unemployment. Family life will shred, and possibly an army of former truck drivers will enlist with others of the digitally ditched and wreak political havoc. Shippers will sing "Happy Days Are Here Again." For truckers it will be, "Brother Can You Spare a Dime?"

It's clear by now that the fruits of automation, computerization and outsourcing are being reaped by the top 1 percent—in this case, shipping companies and not drivers. The old bell curve with the middle class bloating comfy in the middle is being replaced by what's called the power curve, in which something called the 80/20 rule applies: 20 percent of the participants in an online venture get 80 percent of the rewards. Think Uber. It's not the drivers who are getting rich. Something new and possibly awful is happening.

Many books have been written about this phenomenon, and in 2012, the Aspen Institute convened a meeting on this topic, with the resulting report bearing the jaunty title of "Power-Curve Society: The Future of Innovation, Opportunity and Social Equity in the Emerging Networked Economy." One participant was Kim Taipale, a leading thinker in this field. I quote from the Aspen report on its summary of Taipale's thesis: "The era of bell curve distributions that supported a bulging social middle class is over. ... Education per se is not going to make up the difference."

What will make up the difference? President Obama is giving it a shot by proposing to raise taxes on the very rich and relieve the tax burdens of the middle and lower classes. This makes so much sense that the Republican Party recently rose as one to oppose it, denouncing the proposal, as always, as a nonstarter. The GOP's monomaniacal mantra is always to lower taxes because that supposedly produces jobs (Oh, yeah, where are they?), as well as billionaires. (No problem finding them.)

Many of the jobs currently being produced are part-time and low-wage, but even when the pay is good, the jobs are often evanescent—gone in a year or so.

For the past several weeks I've been accosting captains of industry and asking how the American economy is going to both raise incomes and retain jobs. One told me that the rich are going to have to carry the not-so-rich—a vast and expensive welfare program. Another suggested make-work of the sort that FDR tried during the Depression: goodbye self-service gas stations, welcome back attendants and someone to wipe the windshield.

Still others insist that all this worrying is about nothing particularly new under the sun. The United States and, indeed, the industrialized world, has weathered this sort of thing before—the assembly line replacing all those cool artisans making carriages, horseless or otherwise. New jobs are just over the horizon. Innovation and education will create them. Just you wait and see. The app, as Google's executive chairman Eric Schmidt pointed out in a recent talk, is only six years old.

> **The middle class has flat-lined; unemployment is down but wages aren't up.**

To my ears, the optimists sound Panglossian. I have watched Uber (which I use) chew up the taxi industry. Office buildings are being erected for a new age of fewer employees. The law library is online, the back office is overseas—and steno exists only in old movies. ("Miss Jones, take a letter ... ") The middle class has flat-lined; unemployment is down but wages aren't up.

Much of this is ultimately supposed to be good. The term "disrupter" has become an accolade, like first-responder or something. Yet there could be an awful political and social price to pay, and that, for the moment, is being discussed only in whispers—largely limited to forums like Aspen and not the political arena. The stirring will likely have severe political repercussions. After all, what is being disrupted is not the occasional industry but the American Dream. The disrupters disrupt sleep itself.

### Print Citations

**CMS:** Cohen, Richard. "Technology Disrupting the American Dream." In *The Reference Shelf: The American Dream*, edited by Annette Calzone, 126-127. Ipswich, MA: H.W. Wilson, 2018.

**MLA:** Cohen, Richard. "Technology Disrupting the American Dream." *The Reference Shelf: The American Dream*. Ed. Annette Calzone. Ipswich: H.W. Wilson, 2018. 126-127. Print.

**APA:** Cohen, R. (2018). Technology disrupting the American dream. In Annette Calzone (Ed.), *The reference shelf: The American Dream* (pp. 126-127). Ipswich, MA: H.W. Wilson. (Original work published 2015)

# Is China Leaping Past Us?

By Daniel Kliman and Harry Krejsa
*Politico*, September 11, 2017

Sixty years ago this fall, the Soviet Union shocked the world by launching into orbit Earth's first artificial satellite, Sputnik 1. The beach ball-sized spacecraft was an astounding scientific achievement, one previously thought beyond the reach of Moscow. As Sputnik circled the globe and emitted radio signals detectable by anyone with a short-wave receiver, the American public experienced a crisis of confidence over their country's standing in the world and its Cold War competitiveness.

We know the rest of the story. American scientists and policymakers were shaken out of the complacent assumption that their technological edge was insurmountable. American government, universities, and industry mobilized for a competition of scientific innovation—and won.

In recent months, China has quietly given the United States a series of new "Sputnik Moments"—not as dramatic as a radio beacon from overhead, but just as significant as a challenge to American technological leadership. And as U.S. debates have focused on trade deficits and recovering manufacturing jobs, Beijing has achieved the scientific and technological feats that herald its arrival as an innovation superpower. These "Sputnik Moments" extend across multiple industries, from communications technology to renewable energy. Collectively, they pose a risk to America's future economic dynamism, as well as its military superiority.

This August, China successfully tested the world's first quantum satellite communication—relying on the physics of quantum entanglement to send and receive provably secure messages. While the United States faces a regulatory morass around the world-shaking potential of CRISPR [clustered regular interspaced short palindromic repeats] gene editing technologies, China last year announced seven human trials to treat cancer and other ailments. As coal finds itself again at the center of the American energy policy debate, China's photovoltaic capacity has surged. In just the first six months of 2017, China added new solar energy generation capacity equal to half of the United States' entire installed solar base at the end of 2016.

These largely overlooked "Sputnik Moments" have thus far failed to galvanize a U.S. response.

In fact, they underscore the need for action to sustain America's innovation edge. Improving the quality of the U.S. education system and ensuring sufficient government funding for long-term research and development is essential, but will only succeed if the United States simultaneously addresses China's sweeping and ambitious effort to acquire U.S. technology.

Unlike during the Cold War, today cutting-edge technology development in the United States occurs largely in the commercial sector, and often through cross-border collaboration. This means that technology breakthroughs in the United States can benefit economic competitors—for example, China has built on CRISPR gene editing, which was invented in the United States.

Indeed, Beijing has in recent years benefitted from acquiring U.S. intellectual property to leapfrog traditional research and development costs and timelines. Although the threat of illegal Chinese cyber theft is well known, China is also employing a variety of tools designed to extract U.S. achievements in innovation without having to break any laws or firewalls. These tools range from coercive trade practices to structured corporate finance. For example, in exchange for access to China's massive and fast-growing market, Beijing has required some U.S. companies to trade away their intellectual property or engage in forced joint ventures with local Chinese firms. These shotgun corporate marriages can be little more than involuntary technology transfers imposed on U.S. companies seeking new sources of growth.

In the United States, China has adopted less heavy-handed tactics. Its companies are attempting to acquire U.S. firms in key advanced technology sectors like semiconductor development and manufacturing. Chinese corporations have also opened research centers in the United States to tap American talent, and made early-stage investments in American startups focused on cutting-edge technologies like artificial intelligence and robotics. A small Silicon Valley venture might find access to their intellectual property a minor price to pay for a game-changing capital infusion.

Failing to address China's efforts to acquire U.S. technology will have far-reaching consequences. The Commission on the Theft of American Intellectual Property estimates that piracy, theft, and counterfeiting by China costs the U.S. economy between $225 billion and $600 billion a year, or up to 3 percent of the entire U.S. GDP. In the long term, the costs only grow more daunting. If scientific advances in quantum communications, artificial intelligence, biotechnology, energy, and battery technology increasingly move to China, so will the future industries—and jobs— that will accompany them. Moreover, future U.S. military advantage depends on America's continued technological leadership. If China outpaces the United States in innovation, loss of America's military edge in the Asia-Pacific, if not globally, could follow.

Much has been made of U.S. efforts to combat cyber-enabled Chinese economic espionage, including the 2015 agreement concluded by the Obama Administration. But leaving aside illegal cyber theft, China can exploit many *legal* vehicles to acquire U.S. technology. As a result, the United States must treat this problem differently than traditional industrial espionage.

This starts with changing how the U.S. government organizes for economic competition. As currently structured, the Committee on Foreign Investment in the United States (CFIUS), a body set up to review foreign investments for national security consequences, is not equipped for the task. CFIUS lacks the resources for its current caseload, and overly focuses on individual transactions rather than larger trends. Smaller transactions—like those early investments in cutting-edge startups—fall below the radar.

In many ways, the U.S. government's current organization for economic competition replicates many of the failures that plagued counterterrorism efforts prior to the September 11th attacks. Expertise, authorities, and information are diffused across the government. This precludes a strategic approach, creates dangerous bureaucratic seams, and hinders swift action to counter a fluid and evolving challenge.

For these reasons, the United States should consider establishing a National Economic Competition Center (NECC) modeled after the National Counterterrorism Center (NCTC). Established in the years following the September 11th attacks, the NCTC was built on the premise that terror threats require swift cooperation across the U.S. government and with a level of information sharing that could not occur absent a centralized, dedicated effort. Like combatting terrorism, safeguarding technological security requires cutting across bureaucratic lines and will depend on both domestically- and internationally-oriented agencies.

> **China is employing a variety of tools designed to extract U.S. achievements in innovation without having to break any laws or firewalls.**

An effective National Economic Competition Center, like the NCTC, would convene key players from relevant agencies such as the Departments of Defense, Commerce, and Treasury, along with the U.S. Trade Representative, the Federal Bureau of Investigations, and the rest of the intelligence community. It would pool information from across the government, and leverage big data to track Chinese efforts to acquire U.S. technology.

The National Economic Competition Center would also play a decisive role in CFIUS. Possessing the best sight picture on China's economic activities, it would review CFIUS recommendations involving Chinese firms and wield a veto over decisions by the current membership. The NECC would also recommend technologies requiring additional scrutiny by CFIUS, and in cases involving Chinese companies, monitor compliance with CFIUS mitigation agreements, which commit parties in a transaction to taking special actions to address national security concerns.

A National Economic Competition Center could also serve as a repository for pooling information from firms targeted by China's efforts to acquire their intellectual property. It could function as a one-stop resource for companies under pressure by China to trade away their intellectual property, and recommend policy actions to give U.S. companies the backing they need. In addition, the director of the NECC would regularly meet with technology industry CEOs and Silicon Valley venture capitalists to ensure the U.S. government strikes the right balance between protecting America's technology edge and maintaining the level of openness required for the U.S. innovation ecosystem to thrive.

Recalling that U.S.-Soviet technological rivalry contributed to the modern age through space exploration, materials science, and advanced computing, the United States should boldly embrace economic competition with China. Now is the time to organize to win.

The alternative is to continue on the present course—one in which China leverages America's technology to ultimately become the world leader in innovation.

## Print Citations

**CMS:** Kliman, Daniel, and Harry Krejsa. "Is China Leaping Past Us?" In *The Reference Shelf: The American Dream*, edited by Annette Calzone, 128-131. Ipswich, MA: H.W. Wilson, 2018.

**MLA:** Kliman, Daniel, and Harry Krejsa. "Is China Leaping Past Us?" *The Reference Shelf: The American Dream*. Ed. Annette Calzone. Ipswich: H.W. Wilson, 2018. 128-131. Print.

**APA:** Kliman D., & Krejsa, H. (2018). Is China leaping past us? In Annette Calzone (Ed.), *The reference shelf: The American Dream* (pp. 128-131). Ipswich, MA: H.W. Wilson. (Original work published 2017)

# Cities Are Killing the Future of Work (and the American Dream)

By Stephane Kasriel
*Fast Company*, January 18, 2018

Today Amazon announced that it's whittled down more than 230 applicants to a shortlist of 20 places where it will build a second headquarters, dubbed "HQ2." With up to 50,000 new high-skilled jobs and $5 billion of investment at stake, the contest has been fierce, with cities, counties, and states all competing to offer a $530-billion company what's likely to be an extraordinarily lavish package of tax incentives.

It comes as no surprise that the 20 finalists are all big, educated, and prosperous urban hubs, or else nearby suburbs within close commuting distances to large cities. Los Angeles, Chicago, Toronto, Atlanta, and Maryland's Montgomery County (just over the Potomac from Washington, D.C.) are all in the running.

This should have us worried. The same economic development playbook that's driving competition for HQ2 seems less and less sustainable. Over the last decade, our obsession with luring large corporate offices toward increasingly dense central business districts has strained American life as we know it—particularly for the younger half of the workforce. For too many cities, being an engine of fast-paced, high-skilled job growth has also meant higher rents, longer commutes, less savings, and fewer homeowners.

If we're going to build a future of work that's secure, innovative, and equitable, we're going to need to buck one of the fastest-growing global trends: the urbanization of work.

## Clustering Ourselves into a Corner

This isn't an impossible problem to solve. We need to start generating work where people live, and there's never been a better time for it. Technological advances–think widespread videoconferencing apps, a growing freelance labor pool, and the proliferation of coworking spaces and collaboration software–combined with rise of the knowledge economy offer alternatives to a 1950s-style work-here-live-there paradigm.

Not long after the internet went mainstream, many predicted remote and virtual workplaces would soon be the norm. And as our digital lives expanded in the early

2000s, it made sense to believe that a company's physical office was nearing obsolescence, at least for the post-industrial economy's growing knowledge workers.

Yet in 2018, place remains all-important. Sure, more people are working from home these days than ever before, but the growth of remote work has been slower than expected. According to the Bureau of Labor Statistics, the share of workers who performed some of their work from home rose only five percentage points in the 12 years between 2003 and 2015 (from 19% to 24%). A major reason is the clustering of high-tech industries in urban areas, with mini Silicon Valleys appearing all over North America, from the Vancouver-Seattle region to the Boston-Providence corridor. Indeed, much of the post-recession growth in the United States has been driven by two intersecting forces: the dynamics of tech employment and municipal politics.

Facing an acute shortage of the high-skilled talent they need, tech companies—many of which might even be based out in the suburbs, like Facebook and Alphabet—have piled into downtowns in search of more and better talent. That often means poaching from your competitor down the block. Too many companies remain unimaginative about the workforce flexibility that technology offers, and too few big cities want that to change.

City leaders still want bright, shiny symbols of their grandeur, and many are desperate to claim the mantle of "job creator," even if it means deferring tax revenue for generations. As the competition for Amazon's HQ2 reveals, many politicians are willing to give away the bank to make it happen.

## Farther and Farther

The net effect of all these factors has been an unprecedented geographic concentration of jobs—and opportunity. As the U.S. emerged from an economic recovery in the early 1990s, 125 counties created half of all new businesses, according to Census data. Compare that with our most recent economic recovery, which picked up beginning in 2010: just 20 counties have created half of all new businesses.

Then there's the concentration of jobs within cities themselves. Over the last decade, job-growth rates within city centers have outpaced their once-dominant suburbs. This isn't just a New York or San Francisco phenomenon but has also played out elsewhere, from Chicago and Orlando to Charlotte and Milwaukee. In other words, the jobs haven't just gotten farther and farther from folks who live in rural areas. They've even gotten farther from folks who live in cities themselves.

> For too many cities, being an engine of fast-paced, high-skilled job growth has also meant higher rents, longer commutes, less savings, and fewer homeowners.

Consider this 2015 Brookings Institution report, which found that the number of jobs within the typical commute distance for residents of major metro areas fell by 7% between 2000 and 2012; In fact, job opportunities within typical commuting distances shrunk in 67 of the largest 96 metro areas in the U.S.

The consequences of refusing to reimagine where and how we work threatens the American dream as we know it. With rents rising faster than incomes in many major American cities, rates of homeownership–historically one of the main drivers of wealth creation, but not necessarily anymore—hit a 50-year low in mid-2016.

## Go Home Already

This summer, WordPress CEO Matt Mullenweg told workers in his posh 14,000-square-foot San Francisco office to go home and not come back. He wasn't firing everybody. Instead, the CEO of the popular publishing platform was inviting his employees to do their work wherever they wanted, and promising he'd help them do it.

Mullenweg has completely reorganized his 550-person, $1-billion company around working remotely. Employees now get stipends to set up home offices. When they have meetings, they do it in online chatrooms. And when work does really require some face time, WordPress pays the costs for them to meet up.

Earlier this year, Zapier's CEO Wade Foster told his tech company's employees, many of whom were struggling to make ends meet in the San Francisco metro area, that he'd pay them up to $10,000 to move somewhere else. "It can be a real challenge to turn the Bay Area into a lifelong home rather than a short stop somewhere in our twenties and thirties," Foster, who's originally from central Missouri, explained to his workers in a blog post last March.

"The housing crunch and high cost of living simply price out many families and, despite loving the area, the realities are many of us need to look elsewhere to create the life we want for our families." (While Zapier tells *Fast Company* that applications have grown 53% as of last October since the "de-location" offer was announced, two Bay Area employees have been hired but no one at the company has yet taken Foster up on it.)

Zapier is one of a handful of companies that is 100% remote; it's published a downloadable guide showing other executives how to do the same. Buffer ditched its offices for a completely distributed workforce two years ago, and while GitHub keeps a few physical workspaces for those who want to show up, it has also allowed its employees to work wherever they want for years, even renting coworking spaces around the world for in-person collaboration.

The freedom to work from anywhere is also one major factor cited by the growing number of freelancers. With more than 57 million Americans having freelanced this year, 45% say that being able to work where they want allows them to live in a less expensive area than a traditional job, according to my company Upwork's latest *Freelancing in America* report. And finally, we have the technology to do what previous rounds of innovation haven't: The proliferation of coworking spaces, faster and more widely available broadband (even despite the roiling net-neutrality wars), the growing popularity of video chat and collaboration platforms, and the promise of virtual and augmented reality are all ways to reinvent work outside of the cities that threaten to stifle it.

But before we can embrace these geographic freedoms, first we need to update our industrial-era mind-set. We no longer work *how* we used to. We shouldn't all be working *where* we're used to, either.

## Print Citations

**CMS:** Kasriel, Stephane. "Cities Are Killing the Future of Work (and the American Dream)." In *The Reference Shelf: The American Dream*, edited by Annette Calzone, 132-135. Ipswich, MA: H.W. Wilson, 2018.

**MLA:** Kasriel, Stephane. "Cities Are Killing the Future of Work (and the American Dream)." *The Reference Shelf: The American Dream*. Ed. Annette Calzone. Ipswich: H.W. Wilson, 2018. 132-135. Print.

**APA:** Kasriel, S. (2018). Cities are killing the future of work (and the American dream). In Annette Calzone (Ed.), *The reference shelf: The American Dream* (pp. 132-135). Ipswich, MA: H.W. Wilson. (Original work published 2018)

# American Innovation Is in Trouble

By Fareed Zakaria
*The Washington Post*, **January 1, 2015**

The world is impressed with the United States these days. On recent trips to Europe and Asia, I kept hearing praise of the country's innovation and entrepreneurship. But a set of new studies suggests that the glittering examples of Facebook, Snapchat and Uber are deceptive. American innovation is in trouble.

"Over the past 30 years, the rate of start-up formation in the United States has slowed markedly, and the technology industry has come to be dominated by older companies," writes Robert Litan in the current issue of *Foreign Affairs*. In 1978, start-ups—companies less than a year old — made up almost 15 percent of all U.S. companies. But by 2011, that figure had slumped to 8 percent. "For the first time in three decades, business deaths exceeded business births," notes Litan.

U.S. companies are also getting older. Litan notes that "the proportion of U.S. companies considered mature, meaning at least 16 years old, rose from 23 percent of all firms in 1992 to 34 percent in 2011." The problem with this trend is that, historically, older firms are more risk-averse, rigid and incrementally innovative than young ones.

Litan's solutions are sensible and bipartisan: Let in more talented immigrants who combine technological prowess with an appetite for risk — and who are disproportionately likely to start new firms. Regularly review and thin out regulations that make it difficult for the average person to start a company. Make it easier for people to raise money for their ideas over the Internet. And maintain near-universal health care so that people can risk leaving an established company without worrying about their family's health.

Innovation is partly about entrepreneurship but also about technology. And there are some, such as billionaire entrepreneur Peter Thiel, who argue that, despite the hype, we don't actually live in innovative times. Founders Fund, Thiel's venture capital firm, put it pithily: "We wanted flying cars, instead we got 140 characters," referring to Twitter.

I think there's strong evidence that information technology has been utterly transforming and will continue to transform, moving into industries such as health care and education. But my worry is that the rise of IT was the fruit of many years of investment. We are eating seed corn but not laying the groundwork for the next great technological revolutions.

If you ask people in Silicon Valley what makes it work, they will talk about many things — the ability to fail, the lack of hierarchy, the culture of competition. One

**China is on track to surpass the United States in spending on research and development.**

thing almost no one mentions is the government. And yet, the Valley's origins are deeply tied to government support. The reason there were so many engineers in California in the 1950s and 1960s was because large defense companies had attracted them there. Most of the legendary start-ups that fueled the computer revolution — Fairchild Semiconductor, Intel — got off the ground largely because the military, and later NASA, would buy their products until they became cheap and accessible enough for the broader commercial market. GPS, the technology that now powers the information revolution, was developed for the military.

And then there was government funding for research, which is sometimes thought of simply as large grants to universities for basic science but often was far more ingenious. My favorite example comes from Walter Isaacson's fascinating new book, *The Innovators*. In the 1950s, the U.S. government funded a massive project at MIT's Lincoln Laboratory, employing equal numbers of psychologists and engineers who worked together to find ways "that humans could interact more intuitively with computers and information could be presented with a friendlier interface." Isaacson traces how this project led directly to the user-friendly computer screens of today as well as ARPANET, the precursor of the Internet.

Federal funding for basic research and technology should be utterly uncontroversial. It has been one of the greatest investments in human history. And yet it has fallen to its lowest level as a percentage of GDP in four decades. Meanwhile, the rest of the world is catching up in entrepreneurship and research. A real start-up culture is emerging in Sweden, Israel, Beijing and Bangalore. China is on track to surpass the United States in spending on research and development.

But there is hope. Ajay Piramal, a thoughtful Indian businessman, said to me, "I think one of the reasons that the United States is so successful is that it constantly criticizes itself. All that criticism makes sure that you never get complacent." So while foreigners praise U.S. innovation today, Americans should set about making sure that there is innovation tomorrow as well.

## Print Citations

**CMS:** Zakaria, Fareed. "American Innovation Is in Trouble." In *The Reference Shelf: The American Dream*, edited by Annette Calzone, 136-138. Ipswich, MA: H.W. Wilson, 2018.

**MLA:** Zakaria, Fareed. "American Innovation Is in Trouble." *The Reference Shelf: The American Dream*. Ed. Annette Calzone. Ipswich: H.W. Wilson, 2018. 136-138. Print.

**APA:** Zakaria, F. (2018). American innovation is in trouble. In Annette Calzone (Ed.), *The reference shelf: The American Dream* (pp. 136-138). Ipswich, MA: H.W. Wilson. (Original work published 2015)

# The Ugly Truth about America's Economy in Just Four Words

By Linette Lopez
*Business Insider*, October 1, 2017

The ugliest truth about America's future can be summed up in four words: There is no plan.

Americans know this, but we haven't really taken it seriously. In 2017, Democrats live in hopes that the meager policy arguments and "plans" Republicans put out into the ether never make it out of Congress. Republicans are the ones putting out these thin arguments and watching them wilt, much to their embarrassment. Most everyone else just wants the President to stop tweeting.

We're all living in the moment, waiting for it to pass.

But the problem with that short-termism is that having no plan means we are stagnating as a nation.

- We do not have a real plan for health care, and costs continue to gobble up American wages.

- We do not have a plan for dealing with globalization and economic change, but that change continues to shape our economy.

- We don't have a plan to update our decrepit infrastructure.

- The one plan we did have—the Federal Reserve's post-financial crisis program—is about to be unwound, marking the end of the last clear, executable plan to bolster America's economy.

There's been a question floating around Wall Street since Trump was elected. Why does hard economic data show that our economic situation is deteriorating, while the soft data shows that we all feel like everything is doing fine?

It's because the data is looking at our reality, and when we think about the economy, we don't feel like doing the same. Call us optimistic, but some Americans mistakenly think that certain tweaks alone—tax reform here, getting rid of Obamacare there—can bring prosperity. But we're too far gone for that, we need what George H.W. Bush in 1987 derisively called "the vision thing."

When you choose to look at the future—an exercise that we as a nation have chosen to avoid for the last 30-some years—you realize that we've come to a point where our complacency has consequences. We've come to the point where we desperately need a plan. And there is no plan.

## You Can't Fight China's Plan with No Plan

I could illustrate this in a bunch of ways, but—for now—I choose our economic relationship with the world.

Earlier this month I was in the ballroom at The Pierre Hotel in New York with hundreds of Wall Street suits listening to lectures and watching how this plan vacuum is bubbling up to bother even the richest Americans.

On stage were Jim Breyer, the billionaire CEO of Breyer Capital—a California venture capital firm that invested in companies like Facebook early—and Tom Siebel, founder of software company C3 IoT. They were talking about future things: investing in technology, artificial intelligence, economic warfare.

Now of course, when you talk about that kind of thing in 2017, you have to talk about China—the world's number 2 economy nipping at America's heels.

"We are not actually going into China," said Siebel. Here's what else he said (emphasis is mine).

> We are visited by a Chinese company every week, by State Grid, South China Grid, we were visited this week, by China Mobile and so we're kind of swarmed by the Chinese... it is probably a third of the market opportunity globally as it relates to this space. But basically, what's going on in China, due to the mandates of the 12th and 13th five-year plan, and I know this is politically incorrect, but I don't offer political correctness, is *a massive, state-sanctioned intellectual property theft*.

Breyer didn't disagree, he merely added that the Chinese government's investment in achieving its goals in the technology space has led to some amazing investments for his firm. That, plus the country's massive population, is what has made investing in China a must-do for US multinational corporations for years now.

"It is only accelerating," Breyer said, "and so for consumer internet applications both in the urban areas and now the rapidly modernizing rural areas, it's such an enormous financial opportunity that from an investment standpoint, when I think where are the great opportunities where we can generate tremendous alpha, it is in Chinese deep technology companies that are focused on the Chinese market."

But as Siebel responded: "These are not mutually exclusive statements. I am certain that is true."

And there it is, the double-edged sword—damned if you do in China, damned if you don't.

China has a plan to overtake America, and American business has only helped it. Conversely, our government doesn't have a plan for China. The promise of China's massive market has been too tantalizing an opportunity for businesses to pass up, so they've set up joint ventures in China, opened offices, and subjected themselves to all of the invasions and surveillance of China's Big Brother state.

Now they're upset that their ideas are being stolen. But what did they expect? They knew where they were going. They just didn't have a plan for how to protect themselves once they got there.

## Bullying Is Not a Policy: It Is Also Not a Plan

Of course, we can't blame this entirely on American business. The government should take some of the blame as well. Until earlier this month, the Treasury's Committee on Foreign Investment (CIFIUS) —the body that determines whether or not an American company can sell itself to a foreign company—was barely active.

Earlier this month, though, CIFIUS blocked the sale of Lattice Semiconductor, a California-based company, to a Chinese hedge fund. This is just barely a good start to filtering what we sell to our competitor-nation, where the state and business are often interchangeable. But that's basically where the good things end when it comes to Trump administration ideas for dealing with China and globalization in general.

US trade representative Robert Lighthizer, a throwback to the Reagan era before the World Trade Organization (WTO) existed, is pretty angry about this. Earlier this month he called China's threat "unprecedented," and this summer the White House initiated a hyper-aggressive, pre-WTO style investigation into China's IP threat. If the country is found to be stealing

> **Our globalization policy is right now a series of grandstands on the world stage.**

US intellectual property, the government could work around the WTO and slap tariffs on China unilaterally in about a year. That would shock the world, and it could also start a trade war.

This is a one-off, not a China strategy or plan. Even if it was, it wouldn't be a good plan.

But that's what our trade policy—so, ostensibly, our globalization policy—is right now—a series of grandstands on the world stage.

We're picking apart NAFTA and grandstanding over auto parts. We're picking fights with Canadians over airplanes (another thing that could start a trade war in a year). We're heckling our friends in the EU over steel . We're pretending we're above the WTO because we can throw our might around in trade negotiations—that is, except for when we're talking about China. Lighthizer, during that same discussion, mentioned that working with the WTO is fine in that case.

What that tells you, is that we can't bully the number 2 economy in the world. And we'll only use institutions meant to put countries on equal footing when we can't bully. This smacks horribly of a country so clumsily playing defense, that offense is beyond its grasp.

Another example of this from Lighthizer's talk. The United States needs to nominate two judges to the WTO's appellate body for dispute settlement—often called "the crown jewel of the international system." Right now it has three, the minimum number it needs to operate.

Lighthizer has objected to nominating judges for some procedural reasons, but the reality is, as he said in his talk, he longs for the days before the WTO. Back then we had the General Agreement on Tariffs and Trade (GATT) and things were more chaotic—disputes were settled through diplomacy, not a fixed set of rules and impartial judgment. It meant that the strongest country often won.

And that's what Lighthizer likes, and so he's willing to just let the WTO languish where he can, creating chaos.

This isn't a way to prosperity, it's a way to start a fight. None of this will permanently bring jobs back to America. None of this will prepare our workforce for the jobs of the future. None of this will encourage American businesses to invest more in meaningful strategies for the future rather than stock buybacks.

## No Plan-istan

A few months ago I texted a Wall Street source—one of those billionaire types that could live everywhere and nowhere if he wanted to—and asked him if this China IP issue worried him.

And shocker. From somewhere in South Beach he told me that the consequences of that would be a year and a half away—and so, of course, he wasn't worried.

You see, that's how the stock market works. It is, as ever, a marker of how people in the present think of the future, and not the future itself. This has exposed a staggering disconnect between the high stock prices and what people think of the market's eerie march ever higher.

"I have absolutely no idea. I cannot for the life of me understand why the market keeps going up," billionaire businessman Michael Bloomberg told CBS in an interview this week. "Our economy has some real challenges. The infrastructure's falling apart. We're destroying jobs with technology. We are keeping the best and the brightest from around the world [from] coming to America to create new jobs and create new businesses. All of those things would give you pause to worry about the future."

They would, of course, but only if you allow them to.

But no one wants to be worried, it's better to think short term if you're looking for a reason to buy. A week before Bloomberg voiced his concern there was worry at Delivering Alpha.

"I'm not happy when I think of what's coming," said Michael Trotsky, Chief Investment Officer of the Massachusetts Pension Reserves Investment Management. "Returns have been good but risks have increased... debt on [corporate] balance sheets rising."

Healthcare costs will continue to gobble up 1/6th of the economy because we have no plan to rein them in. Tax breaks will help margins, but that's hardly innovation. It's even less a plan. It's certainly not a strategy. Regulatory reform is a blip. It's not going to create the jobs of the future or build new industries. Without that the middle class' purchasing power will continue to shrink, and so will our economy. None of this is a plan. It's not a strategy. It's a short-term stock play at best.

But that's all we can stomach right now, so the market is rallying.

We are not futurists, we are melancholy historians, constantly looking back at a greatness that once was instead of figuring out ways to dominate the future. We're all running. The rich to their tax havens and the poor to their populism. Trump and his band of swamp things and Goldman guys would rather talk about returning to the 1980s than what will happen in the 2020s. CNBC talking heads compare everything in the stock market to 2007, to 1999, to 1987, to whatever keeps them looking backward instead of forward.

Forward is too hard. We have no plan.

## Print Citations

**CMS:** Lopez, Linette. "The Ugly Truth about America's Economy in Just Four Words." In *The Reference Shelf: The American Dream*, edited by Annette Calzone, 139-143. Ipswich, MA: H.W. Wilson, 2018.

**MLA:** Lopez, Linette. "The Ugly Truth about America's Economy in Just Four Words." *The Reference Shelf: The American Dream*. Ed. Annette Calzone. Ipswich: H.W. Wilson, 2018. 139-143. Print.

**APA:** Lopez, L. (2018). The ugly truth about America's economy in just four words. In Annette Calzone (Ed.), *The reference shelf: The American Dream* (pp. 139-143). Ipswich, MA: H.W. Wilson. (Original work published 2017)

# Bibliography

Abadi, Mark. "6 American Work Habits People in Other Countries Think Are Ridiculous." *Independent*. Independent Media. Nov 17, 2017. Retrieved from https://www.independent.co.uk/news/business/american-work-habits-us-countries-job-styles-hours-hoilday-a8060616.html.

Aizenman, Nurith. "Mexicans in the U.S. Are Sending Home More Money Than Ever." *NPR*. National Public Radio. Feb 10, 2017. Retrieved from https://www.npr.org/sections/goatsandsoda/2017/02/10/514172676/mexicans-in-the-u-s-are-sending-home-more-money-than-ever.

Allen, Katie. "Technology Has Created More Jobs Than It Has Destroyed, Says 140 Years of Data." *The Guardian*. The Guardian News and Media. Aug 18, 2015. Retrieved from https://www.theguardian.com/business/2015/aug/17/technology-created-more-jobs-than-destroyed-140-years-data-census.

"The American Dream." *Merriam-Webster*. Merriam-Webster, Inc. 2018. Retrieved from https://www.merriam-webster.com/dictionary/the%20American%20dream.

Badger, Emily. "Whites Have Huge Wealth Edge Over Blacks (but Don't Know It)." *The New York Times*. The New York Times, Co. Sep 18, 2017. Retrieved from https://www.nytimes.com/interactive/2017/09/18/upshot/black-white-wealth-gap-perceptions.html.

Bouie, Jamelle. "The Wealth Gap Between Whites and Blacks Is Widening." *Slate*. Atlantic Monthly Group. Sep 17, 2017. Retrieved from http://www.slate.com/articles/news_and_politics/politics/2017/09/the_wealth_gap_between_whites_and_blacks_is_widening.html.

Bowman, Karlyn, Marsico, Jennifer K., and Heather Sims. "Public Opinion and the American Dream." *AEI*. American Enterprise Institute. Dec 15, 2014. Retrieved from http://www.aei.org/publication/public-opinion-american-dream/.

Calamur, Krishnadev. "Why Norwegians Aren't Moving to the U.S." *Atlantic*. Atlantic Monthly Group. Jan 12, 2018. Retrieved from https://www.theatlantic.com/international/archive/2018/01/trump-shithole-norway/550382/.

Calfas, Jennifer. "President Trump's Net Worth Tumbled Last Year: Here's What Changed." *Time*. Money. Time Inc. Mar 6, 2018. Retrieved from http://time.com/money/5188095/donald-trump-net-worth-2018/.

Chang, Gordon H., and Shelley Fisher Fishkin. "'The Chinese Helped Build America'." *Forbes*. Forbes Inc. May 12, 2014. Retrieved from https://www.forbes.com/sites/forbesasia/2014/05/12/the-chinese-helped-build-america/#77ab0f7339bc.

"The Chinaman as a Railroad Builder." *Scientific American*. Munn & Company. July 31, 1869, 75.

"Chinese Railroad Workers." *Stanford University*. FAQs. Retrieved from http://web.stanford.edu/group/chineserailroad/cgi-bin/wordpress/faqs/.

Chui, Michael, Manyika, James, and Mehdi Miremadi. "Where Machines Could Replace Humans—and Where They Can't (Yet)." *McKinsey Quarterly*. July 2016. Retrieved from https://www.mckinsey.com/business-functions/digital-mckinsey/our-insights/where-machines-could-replace-humans-and-where-they-cant-yet.

Churchwell, Sarah. "The Great Gatsby and the American Dream." *The Guardian*. The Guardian News and Media. May 25, 2012. Retrieved from https://www.theguardian.com/books/2012/may/25/american-dream-great-gatsby.

Coleman, Arica L. "The Problem with Calling the U.S. a 'Nation of Immigrants'." *Time*. Time Inc. Mar 17, 2017. Retrieved from http://time.com/4705179/nation-of-immigrants-problem/.

Connor, Phillip. "Most Displaced Syrians Are in the Middle East, and about a Million Are in Europe." *Pew Research*. Facttank. Jan 29, 2018. Retrieved from http://www.pewresearch.org/fact-tank/2018/01/29/where-displaced-syrians-have-re-settled/.

Cortright, Joe. "How Housing Intensifies the Racial Wealth Gap." *Citylab*. Atlantic Monthly Group. Sep 22, 2017. Retrieved from https://www.citylab.com/equity/2017/09/how-housing-intensifies-the-racial-wealth-gap/540879/.

Diaz, Thatiana. "U.S. Citizenship Director Who Removed Phrase 'Nation of Immigrants' Is *Actually* Son of Immigrant." *People*. People Inc. Feb 27, 2018. Retrieved from https://people.com/chica/uscis-director-who-changed-mission-statement-is-son-of-peruvian-immigrant/.

DiBacco, Thomas V. "How a History Professor Became a Newspaper Columnist." *Orlando Sentinel*. Tronc, Inc.. Jun 22, 2018. Retrieved from http://www.orlandosentinel.com/opinion/os-ed-history-professor-to-newspaper-columnist-20180612-story.html.

Doyle, Don H. "The Civil War Was Won by Immigrant Soldiers." *Time*. Time Inc. Jun 29, 2015. Retrieved from http://time.com/3940428/civil-war-immigrant-soldiers/.

"Dreams." *BBC Bitesize*. English Literature. GCSE. Retrieved from https://www.bbc.com/education/guides/zpvhycw/revision/2.

"The Dust Bowl." Great Depression and World War I. *LOC*. Library of Congress. 2016. Retrieved from https://www.loc.gov/teachers/classroommaterials/presentationsandactivities/presentations/timeline/depwwii/dustbowl/.

Egan, Matt. "America More Pessimistic Than Poor Nations." *CNN*. CNN Money. Oct 9, 2014. Retrieved from https://money.cnn.com/2014/10/09/news/economy/poor-nations-more-optimistic-than-united-states/index.html.

Florida, Richard. "The Unhappy States of America." *Citylab*. Atlantic Monthly Group. Mar 20, 2018. Retrieved from https://www.citylab.com/life/2018/03/the-unhappy-states-of-america/555800/.

Frank, Jason, and Isaac Kramnick. "What 'Hamilton' Forgets About Hamilton." *The New York Times*. The New York Times Co. Jun 10, 2016. Retrieved from https://www.nytimes.com/2016/06/11/opinion/what-hamilton-forgets-about-alexander-hamilton.html.

Gould, Elise. "The State of American Wages 2017." *EPI*. Economic Policy Institute.

Mar 1, 2018. Retrieved from https://www.epi.org/publication/the-state-of-amer-ican-wages-2017-wages-have-finally-recovered-from-the-blow-of-the-great-re-cession-but-are-still-growing-too-slowly-and-unequally/.

Greenberg, Jonathan. "Trump Lied to Me about His Wealth to Get into the Forbes 400: Here Are the Tapes." *The Washington Post*. The Washington Post Co. Apr 20, 2018. Retrieved from https://www.washingtonpost.com/outlook/trump-lied-to-me-about-his-wealth-to-get-onto-the-forbes-400-here-are-the-tapes/2018/04/20/ac762b08-4287-11e8-8569-26fda6b404c7_story.html?utm_term=.f8f8e474b89e.

Guarino, Ben, Rauhala, Emily, and William Wan. "China Increasingly Challenges American Dominance of Science." *The Washington Post*. The Washington Post Co. Jun 3, 2018. Retrieved from https://www.washingtonpost.com/national/health-science/china-challenges-american-dominance-of-science/2018/06/03/c1e0cfe4-48d5-11e8-827e-190efaf1f1ee_story.html?noredirect=on&utm_term=.8936e99e0226.

Gunn, Dwyer. "How to Give American Workers Fair Wages." *PSmag*. Pacific Standard. Mar 9, 2018. Retrieved from https://psmag.com/economics/how-to-give-american-workers-fair-wages.

Harriot, Michael. "When the Irish Weren't White." *The Root*. Gizmodo Media Group. Mar 17, 2018. Retrieved from https://www.theroot.com/when-the-irish-weren-t-white-1793358754.

Hess, Edward D. "Will Business Leaders Save the American Dream?" *Medium*. Medium Retrieved from https://medium.com/@edhess33/will-business-leaders-save-the-american-dream-e4d50380d2db.

"James Truslow Adams Papers, 1918-1949." *Columbia University Libraries*. Archival Collections. 2018. Retrieved from http://www.columbia.edu/cu/lweb/archival/collections/ldpd_4078384/.

Kirby, Jen. "Trump Wants Fewer Immigrants from 'Shithole Countries' and More from Places Like Norway." *Vox*. Vox Media. Jan 11, 2018. Retrieved from https://www.vox.com/2018/1/11/16880750/trump-immigrants-shithole-countries-nor-way.

Krogstad, Jens Manuel. "One-in-Four Native Americans and Alaska Native Are Living in Poverty. *Pew Research*. Pew Research Center. Jun 13, 2014. Retrieved from    http://www.pewresearch.org/fact-tank/2014/06/13/1-in-4-native-ameri-cans-and-alaska-natives-are-living-in-poverty/.

Lisca, Peter. "Of Mice and Men." In Hobby, Blake, ed. *The American Dream*. New York: Bloom's Literary Criticism, 2009.

Massie, Victoria M. "Native Americans Like Renee Davis Are Ignored When Police Brutality Is Viewed as Black and White." *Vox*. Vox Media. Oct 25, 2016. Retrieved from https://www.vox.com/identities/2016/10/25/13403290/renee-davis-police-violence-native-american.

McElvaine, Robert S. *The Great Depression: American, 1929-1941.*" New York: Times Books, 1993.

McIntosh, Peggy. "White Privilege and Male Privilege: A Personal Account of

Coming to See Correspondences Through Work in Women's Studies (1988). *Collegeart*. College Art Association of America, Inc. Retrieved from http://www.collegeart.org/pdf/diversity/white-privilege-and-male-privilege.pdf.

"Nearly 6 Million Workers Employed at Immigrant-Owned Businesses, New Report Finds." *New American Economy*. Research Fund. Oct 11, 2016. Retrieved from https://research.newamericaneconomy.org/report/nearly-6-million-workers-employed-at-immigrant-owned-businesses-new-report-finds/.

Nowrasteh, Alex. "The 14 Most Common Arguments against Immigration and Why They're Wrong." *Cato Institute*. Cato at Liberty. May 2, 2018. Retrieved from https://www.cato.org/blog/14-most-common-arguments-against-immigration-why-theyre-wrong.

O'Neil, Eleanor. "Immigration Issues: Public Opinion on Family Separation, DACA, and a Border Wall." *AEI*. American Enterprise Institute. Jun 21, 2018. Retrieved from https://www.aei.org/publication/immigration-issues-public-opinion-on-family-separation-daca-and-a-border-wall/.

Oliphant, Baxter. "Views about Whether Whites Benefit from Societal Advantages Split Sharply along Racial and Partisan Lines." *Pew Research*. Pew Research Center. Sep 28, 2017. Retrieved from http://www.pewresearch.org/fact-tank/2017/09/28/views-about-whether-whites-benefit-from-societal-advantages-split-sharply-along-racial-and-partisan-lines/.

Pappas, Stephanie. "US and France More Depressed Than Poor Countries." *Lifescience*. Purch Media. Jul 25, 2011. Retrieved from https://www.livescience.com/15225-global-depression-poor-rich-countries.html.

"The Partisan Divide on Political Views Grows Even Wider." *Pew Research*. Pew Research Center. Oct 5, 2017. Retrieved from http://www.people-press.org/2017/10/05/4-race-immigration-and-discrimination/.

"Public Trust in Government: 1958-2017." *Pew Research*. Pew Research Center. Dec 14, 2017. Retrieved from http://www.people-press.org/2017/12/14/public-trust-in-government-1958-2017/.

Roe, David. "Why Artificial Intelligence Will Create More Jobs Than It Destroys." *CMS Wire*. Simpler Media Group, Inc. Jan 9, 2018. Retrieved from https://www.cmswire.com/digital-workplace/why-artificial-intelligence-will-create-more-jobs-than-it-destroys/.

Rothman, Joshua. "The Origins of 'Priviledge'." *The New Yorker*. Condé Nast. May 12, 2014. Retrieved from https://www.newyorker.com/books/page-turner/the-origins-of-privilege.

"Scandinavian Immigration." *Harvard University Library*. Open Collections Program. Immigration to the United States, 1789-1930." Retrieved from http://ocp.hul.harvard.edu/immigration/scandinavian.html.

Singletary, Michelle. "Black Homeownership Is as Low as It Was When Housing Discrimination Was Legal." *The Washington Post*. The Washington Post Co. Apr 5, 2018. Retrieved from https://www.washingtonpost.com/news/get-there/wp/2018/04/05/black-homeownership-is-as-low-as-it-was-when-housing-discrimination-was-legal/?utm_term=.4044198321ce.

Solman, Paul. "Analysis: If You're Rich, You're More Lucky Than Smart: And There's Math to Prove It." *PBS News Our*. Nine Network. May 15, 2018. Retrieved from https://www.pbs.org/newshour/economy/making-sense/analysis-if-youre-rich-youre-more-lucky-than-smart-and-theres-math-to-prove-it.

Szalavitz, Maia. "What's Behind Rich People Pretending to Be Self-Made?" *The Guardian*. The Guardian News and Media. Jan 29, 2018. Retrieved from https://www.theguardian.com/us-news/2018/jan/29/rich-people-wealth-america.

Thompson, Derek. "How Immigration Became So Controversial." *The Atlantic*. The Atlantic Monthly Group. Feb 2, 2018. Retrieved from https://www.theatlantic.com/politics/archive/2018/02/why-immigration-divides/552125/.

"Transcript of Alien and Sedition Acts (1798)." *Our Documents*. Yale University Library. Retrieved from https://www.ourdocuments.gov/doc.php?flash=false&doc=16&page=transcript.

Vandiver, David. "What Is the Great Gatsby Curve?" *Obamawhitehouse*. The White House. Jun 11, 2013. Retrieved from https://obamawhitehouse.archives.gov/blog/2013/06/11/what-great-gatsby-curve.

Widmer, Ted. "What the Man Behind the 'American Dream' Really Meant." *Boston Globe*. Boston Globe Media Partners, LLC. Apr 16, 2015. Retrieved from https://www.bostonglobe.com/ideas/2015/04/16/what-man-behind-american-dream-really-meant/uni438RcM82Y3QDnkwRz5H/story.html.

Wills, Matthew, "James Truslow Adams: Dreaming Up the American Dream." *Jstory Daily*. JSTOR. May 18, 2015. Retrieved from https://daily.jstor.org/james-truslow-adams-dreaming-american-dream/.

Zeitz, Joshua. "The Real History of American Immigration." *Politico Magazine*. Politico. Aug 6, 2017. Retrieved from https://www.politico.com/magazine/story/2017/08/06/trump-history-of-american-immigration-215464.

Zeitz, Joshua. "When America Hated Catholics." *Politico*. Politico Magazine. Sep 23, 2015. Retrieved from https://www.politico.com/magazine/story/2015/09/when-america-hated-catholics-213177.

# Websites

### American Enterprise Institute
*www.aei.org*

The American Enterprise Institute is a conservative Washington D.C.-based think tank that conducts research on economics, social, and political policy. Developed in the 1930s, the organization identifies and funds research and provides original policy promoting conservative political and economic policies.

### Brookings Institution
*www.brookings.edu*

The Brookings Institution is a Washington D.C.-based policy think tank that supports and publishes research on governmental policy, economics, and development. Established in 1916, Brookings is one of the nation's oldest and most renowned policy research organizations. The Brookings website provides articles and original research on a variety of subjects.

### Center on Budget and Policy Priorities
*www.cbpp.org*

The Center on Budget and Policy Priorities is a Washington-based think tank that supports research into federal and state economic policies. The organization's chief goal is to ensure that policymakers are provided with data on the challenges of low-income families. The organization publishes studies on income inequality, the wealth gap, and a number of other social economic issues.

### Economic Policy Institute (EPI)
*www.epi.org*

The Economic Policy Institute is a Washington-based think tank focused on addressing the needs of low- and middle-income workers. A progressive organization, the EPI funds and carries our research connected with labor and worker's rights and advocates for policies to address income inequality or to benefit low- and middle-income families and workers.

### James M. and Cathleen D. Stone Center on Socio-Economic Inequality
*www.gc.cuny.edu/stonecenter*

The Stone Center is an academic organization, through the City University of New York, dedicated to exploring the issue of income inequality, promoting policy initiatives, and supporting economic and social policy research. The organization's website provides data on income inequality and links to relevant research.

### National Bureau of Economic Research

*www.nber.org*

The National Bureau of Economic Research (NBER) is a national nonprofit research organization that conducts research on the American economy. NBER is one of the most prestigious and largest economic research organizations in the country and helps to create policy recommendations for state and local governments.

### Pew Research Center

*www.pewresearch.org*

Pew Research Center is a nonprofit, nonpartisan think tank based in Washington, D.C. The organization conducts public opinion polling and compiles and funds demographic research. Pew Research has produced numerous studies and conducted many opinion polls on issues related to the American dream and the way that public opinion on this aspect of American culture has changed over time.

### Urban Institute

*www.urban.org*

The Urban Institute is an economic and policy think tank based in Washington D.C. Established in the late 1960s, the Urban Institute is known as one of the premier organizations studying metropolitan politics and economics. The Urban Institute provides articles and original publications on a variety of policy issues.

# Index